Life

of

Libby

Chasing Peace & Justice with Humor, Guts, & Passion

Libby Frank

with

Heather Shafter

Dedication

To members of the Women's International League for Peace & Freedom who helped strengthen my independence; to the inspiring peace and justice activists of today, often led by young Black and brown women; to the Jewish thinkers and activists who helped me blend my heritage and my politics; to my husband, Mort, who has been my lifetime stalwart loving, support, and sons, Alan and Reuben, who (I think) accepted our non-traditional and challenging family life; and to the future—my grandchildren, Stephanie, Julian and Sophie; and all the world's children.

World Youth Song

One great vision unites us
Though remote be the lands of our birth
Foes may threaten and smite us
Still we live to bring peace to the earth.

Every country and nation, stirs with youth's
  inspiration
Young folks are singing, happiness bringing
Friendship to all the world.

Everywhere the youth is singing freedom's song,
  freedom's song
We rejoice to show the world that we are
  strong. We are strong.
We are the youth
And the world acclaims our song of truth
Everywhere the youth is singing freedom's song
Freedom's song, freedom's song.

Contents

Introduction

I first met Libby Frank over 20 years ago. I had graduated from college with a major in Women's Studies and French. During college I had two internships with the Women's International League for Peace and Freedom: one in Philadelphia and one in Paris. After graduation, I found a job with the Philadelphia Corporation for Aging, but the job left me unfulfilled. I missed working on the peace and justice issues within WILPF. So, I attended a local branch meeting, and I met Libby there.

Like Libby, I wanted to leave the world better than I found it, but unlike Libby I was unsure of how to do it. Libby was a natural mentor. She asked me about what I wanted to do in the peace and justice movement, and when I didn't know, she promptly recruited me to the Middle East Committee. As we worked together on the Committee, I got to know more of Libby's story; I was both fascinated and inspired. Over the years, Libby supported racial equality and desegregation, the rights of workers, equal treatment for women, and a just peace in the Middle East. Early on in her work, Libby recognized the intersectionality of all forms of oppression.

In the course of a conversation she might say, "When I went to the World Youth Festival in Germany . . ." or "When I hosted Jane Fonda for the Peace Center . . ." or "That was on my second delegation to the Middle East . . ." or "Did I tell you about how I helped Pete Seeger change the lyrics to the Hammer song?"

I wondered how Libby came to spend her life working on these issues. How did this woman of small means travel the world in pursuit of a more just global society? Libby was sharing one of these anecdotes with me over a lunch at the Trolley Car Diner when I said to her, "I'd like to write your story." That was in 2013.

By working with Libby on creating this book, I imagine extending her mentorship to all its readers. This is not just an individual odyssey, but a look at what it means to have a life-long commitment to making the world better. Many people have a similar aspiration, but like me, have trouble imagining how to do it. Most of us need to earn a living, maintain a household, and care for family members—in addition to any social action. Libby is a model of how to do it. She is not a superhero, but an unassuming hero who we can emulate in our own ways. If this book inspires people to *consistently* take one small action at a time, then we will all contribute to a shared legacy of leaving the world better than we found it.

Heather Shafter

Prologue

I was born in McKeesport, PA, but my family was always moving around because my father couldn't find a steady job. It wasn't until I got older that I realized it was because of the Depression and wasn't necessarily his fault.

After living briefly in Allentown, we settled in Inwood, Long Island in New York for a couple years. We rented the upstairs level of a house owned by an Italian family who lived on the first floor. John and Grace had four children: Alfred, Susie, Julia, and Junior. My mother and Grace were civil to each other but showed no real friendliness. It was a different story with me and Julia. She was only one year older than I was, and we became good friends.

My friendship with Julia gave me my first experience with a different culture and religion. When she went to Catholic Sunday school, I wanted to go, too—and my mother gave me permission. Unfortunately, it was short-lived because my father forbade it when he found out. I found other opportunities to learn with her though.

Every summer a man with a whimsical trailer—much like the Wizard of Oz cart—set himself up at a site near our school. Once a week he taught Italian to the neighborhood kids. Julia and I often went together. We climbed in with the other kids and sat on benches along the sides of his trailer. He taught us a few words each week and the following week he would review them. One week, he asked if anyone remembered how to say "mother." No one remembered except me, the only non-Italian there. I had an early interest in languages and though I never spoke much Italian, I did learn French and Hebrew.

•

It was a difficult time for everyone, including Julia's family. They were a family of six, crowded into the first floor of a house so they could make extra money renting out the second floor to my family. One day, Grace lost her temper with Julia in a way that I had never experienced in my own family.

Julia's family grew grapevines in the backyard to make wine. We liked to spend time back there in the summer because it was shaded and cool. That day, I was chatting with Julia while she handwashed the laundry in a large washtub. She was washing vigorously, creating a mountain of suds. When Grace came out of the house, she saw the bubbles and concluded Julia had used too much soap. Then she *beat* her for using too much soap! I was shocked by the sudden violence. My parents never beat me, even when I made mistakes.

•

One time I was carrying home a bottle of milk and a box of Rice Krispies from the grocery store down the block. My mother frequently sent me there since I didn't have to cross any streets on the way. My Aunt Nettie and Uncle Manny owned the store (they were actually cousins, but we called them aunt and uncle), so I didn't have to carry any money either; Manny always put it on our tab. On my way home I dropped the milk! It spilled all over the sidewalk. My mother was upset at the waste, but she only scolded me saying, "Couldn't you have dropped the Rice Krispies instead?"

•

Every few months, my mother would save up enough money to buy me a Big Little Book. They were a big thing back then. The books were a few inches square and very thick. I would read the whole thing in one sitting, but I was careful not to let my parents know how fast I read them—I didn't want them to feel bad about the money spent.

•

My mother did an incredible job of keeping us fed and clothed under very difficult circumstances. She was very frugal and knew how to stretch a dollar. She was also a really good baker and cook. When I went home for lunch during the school year, my mother always had lunch ready: egg salad, tuna salad, or peanut butter and jelly sandwiches. She took great pride in being a hardworking wife and mother.

We had a coal burning stove for heat, made of heavy black metal. Somehow a dollar bill fell in there once from my mother's apron pocket and my mother put her hand into the flames to pull it out. It was a lot of money back then and she could not afford to let it burn.

My dad was frequently out of town selling insurance—or trying to. One time he brought me back a small gift: a Minnie Mouse wristwatch. It was so nice to get this surprise, but my mother was upset. She said accusingly, "Why'd you spend money on that?" Here my mother was struggling to feed us, and my father spent money on a frivolous gift for me.

Another time, I somehow saved up 10 cents to get my mother a gift for Mother's Day. I went to the 5-and-10-cent-store and bought a fancy handkerchief with "Mother" embroidered on it. This time my father was angry that I'd spent money on an item he said didn't have any use. It was ironic but reflected our situation at the time. We loved each other but money was so tight.

After my brother Marvin was born in 1934, my family was

separated because my mother got very sick from "women's problems." While she recovered, my brother lived with my mother's sisters in New York, and I stayed in Inwood with my father. Uncle Manny would drive us the two and a half hours to New York on Sundays, where I'd see my little brother. I really missed my mother during these visits and was heartbroken that she wasn't around to watch Marvin learning to walk and talk. Eventually my mother recovered enough to come home, and our whole family was under one roof again.

•

Despite having little money, my parents knew how to have fun. For entertainment, they met up with friends to play cards. On the evenings that they went out, my mother would arrange for Julia to come up and stay with me rather than hiring a babysitter. She gave Julia and me big chunks of chocolate before she left, and we would eat them together in the big double bed. We talked and laughed all evening, but tried to keep quiet because my brother Marvin would already be asleep in the crib close to our bed.

When it was my parents' turn to host the card-playing, my mother defied her long tradition of baking and *bought* Hostess cupcakes. They were chocolate cupcakes with whipped cream down the middle. She served them on a beautiful platter, and everyone enjoyed them. Then one of the women asked how she got the whipped cream inside. My mother, with a straight face, began explaining how she managed that feat. My father started laughing and the scam abruptly ended. Many years later, my father was so well-known for his humor that the men's club of his synagogue invited him to tape his collection of jokes. I still remember him practicing and practicing before the recording date.

•

I had to say goodbye to Julia in 1935 when we moved *back* to McKeesport, where my father's parents owned a small kosher grocery store. My grandfather always had a long list of handwritten IOUs from all of the people who needed to buy groceries but couldn't afford to pay for them at the time (or ever).

My dad wasn't earning any money and we couldn't afford the housing in Inwood, so we went to live with my grandparents. I was around seven years old, and Marvin was around one. I shared a bedroom with my father, mother, and brother upstairs in my grandparents' house, right above the store. I had to share a bed with my brother. Every night my parents made me go upstairs with Marvin and stay with him until he fell asleep. Then I could come back down again until it was my own bedtime.

I should also mention that my Uncle Meyer lived with us, along with Uncle Sam and his wife, Bea, and of course, my grandparents. All of us shared *one* bathroom. It was a lot of people in a very small space.

Every Friday night on Shabbos (Sabbath) we would have dinner in the unheated dining room next to the kitchen. Someone would start the electric fireplace shortly before dinner, but it never got comfortably warm. The men would sing prayers from the traditional *siddur*, a prayer book, and then my grandmother served the meal; soup, chicken, and my favorite, *nahit*, which is a dish made with chickpeas, schmaltz, and pepper. It wasn't a lively affair, but I remember those nights with my family fondly.

Despite everything, I was never hungry. Our family was poor while I was growing up, but I never felt insecure. That feeling of security gave me the freedom to be independent—in my thinking and my actions. My independence meant pushing the boundaries of what was expected and what was accepted to be true. As the well-known saying by Laurel Thatcher Ulrich goes, "Well-behaved women seldom make history."

Part 1

Racial Equality, Folk Music, and Communism

Important Work
To Be Done

When the worst of the Depression was finally over, my Uncle Morris somehow got hold of a bunch of money. No one in the family seemed to know how, but he used the money to start a business selling and maintaining slot machines: laundry machines, pinball machines, and other types of coin-operated machines. He hired my father and my Aunt Edith, his sister, so our family packed up and moved from McKeesport to Cleveland, Ohio.

In 1937, we moved to a poor neighborhood on what was considered the wrong side of the tracks. I didn't have a bedroom. I slept inside a cubby hole-type bed near the entrance to the apartment. At least it wasn't with my brother. Oliver Wendell Holmes Elementary School was a short walk away on the other side of the tracks—the "good" side. The school, reflecting the neighborhood, was predominantly Jewish and Black.

By the time I was in high school, we had "moved up" several blocks to the good side of the tracks. This second apartment in Cleveland was nicer with two bedrooms, a good-sized kitchen, and a living room. We lived there for many years. After Holmes Elementary School, I went to Patrick Henry Junior High, and then Glenville High School.

Like the other schools I attended in Cleveland, Glenville High was considerably integrated for the time, but that reality was not always reflected in people's attitudes. I took an honors class with a creative and liberal English teacher named Sidney Vincent. We studied Shakespeare's play, *Othello*. Mr. Vincent told us we were the only high school class in the country to study it. It was considered too controversial; and did provoke discussions about race. One day Mr. Vincent asked the class, "How many of you would not object to living next to a Negro?"

All the students in the class were white. I raised my hand and then looked around the room. A new student was sitting next to me, and her hand was also raised. We were the only ones who raised our hands. I was shocked. It was entirely unexpected that the people I knew, many of them Jewish like me, would feel that way. While the high school was integrated, I had viewed it as much more enlightened than it actually was.

Glenville High was very good academically. Every year, the students scored way above any of the other schools on the citywide tests. The test results from all the city high schools were posted in the hallway so we could see them. Eventually the city stopped giving us the test because they said we were skewing the results!

Unfortunately, our school was as terrible in sports as we were good in academics. One time, the kids called an unofficial rally in the auditorium because our football team had scored. We didn't even win the game, we only scored! When the vice principal found out he got up on the stage and yelled at everyone to go back to class. That may have been my first rally—though many more followed for very different reasons.

I realized early on that there was important work to be done, and that I would help do it. I also had early detractors. As part of a class on "Modern Problems," I completed an assignment about my philosophy of life, which included leaving the world better than I found it.

The teacher, Mr. Thomas, read it aloud to the class and

then declared: "What a load of baloney. You're going to get married and have kids and you're not going to have any effect on the world."

Boy, was he wrong! (Although I did get married and have kids.) I became involved in actions for peace and justice in high school and I never stopped. At that time, I knew that we needed to end segregation and racial inequality. I also recognized that Jewish people needed a safe haven from oppression in Europe. Along with peace, these two issues were my primary focus in the beginning.

During WWII, many of the male students in our class had been drafted and went to war. They were only 18 years old and forced to miss their own high school graduation. *The Cleveland Press* published an op-ed titled *Pollyanna Pep Talks for 1945 Grads Are Out of Place in War-Torn World* that I clipped out and kept.

Dozens of us women had dinner at a Chinese restaurant to celebrate our graduation. None of us had a date because so many of the male graduates were drafted. To be fair, some of us may not have had a date in any case.

Our graduation ceremony was truly unique. Rather than bringing in a commencement speaker, we created our own inspiring message. Our high school paper, *The Glenville Torch*, shared a sneak peak of the event, "It will show how world events and world needs impressed themselves on the consciousness of the class." Rather than just one voice, we wanted a group presentation involving a large part of the class. I helped our commencement committee write and perform a cantata with the theme: the world needs us, and we are coming!

Then we sang our class song, "United Nations on the March":

> United Nations on the March with flag unfurled
> Together fight for victory, a free, new world.

We were determined to defeat Hitler and Mussolini and create a peaceful new world.

Libby Gisser High School Graduation Portrait,
1945, Cleveland.

•

It was special for someone in my family to graduate from high school and I was excited to have some of my cousins from New York attend the ceremony. I didn't plan to stop my education at high school graduation either. It was common in that time to choose between one of two high school tracks:

one to prepare for college and the other for work (the commercial track). Young women in the 1940s did not have many career options. A woman could expect to become a nurse, teacher, or secretary. The mindset was that a career would last until you got married and had kids, after which there'd be no time for a career. The commercial track was more typical for women, but I told my parents that I wanted to take the college track. I knew there was more to learn than what I had acquired in high school. My mother supported my decision, but my father didn't agree. As a compromise, I took typing and shorthand as well as college prep.

It was a good thing I developed typing skills. While I went on to do work other than secretarial, typing jobs helped me earn money for a long time. When I was married and living in Chicago, I got a typing job with *Encyclopedia Britannica*. It was good, steady pay and I learned a lot while working there. At the time, if you bought an encyclopedia set, you could have a certain number of questions answered for free by an *Encyclopedia Britannica* staff person. My job was to type up the answers. The male staffers researched the answers, and the female typists typed them. Often the papers I typed were interesting. One paper I particularly remember explained what some nursery rhymes really meant. One was:

> Baa, baa, black sheep, have you any wool?
> Yes sir, yes sir, three bags full!
> One for the master,
> One for the dame,
> And one for the little boy
> Who lives down the lane.

The verse was a protest about a heavy tax on wool. Most wool went to the Master and Dame and very little was left for the "little boy." Considering my family's financial hardships growing up, this paper was memorable for me.

There was no way our family could pay for tuition and

board at an out-of-town location, so I decided to apply for a scholarship to Cleveland College (part of Western Reserve University). It was in downtown Cleveland and easily accessible by public transportation.

I joined dozens of high school seniors in a school library to interview for scholarships. After a long wait, I was called in and the interviewer asked what I did besides attend school. I told him I taught Hebrew part-time and was active in peace and anti-racism activities. Then he asked what activities I did in my spare time! I could have hit him.

When I got notice I'd be receiving a full scholarship for the first year, I asked if I could postpone it until my senior year, since I knew tuition would rise every year. They laughed off my suggestion and I accepted the scholarship for my first year. I was on my way to developing a global political perspective and speaking out for justice—no matter the consequences.

My Mother Said, "Shh!"

In the fall of 1945, I was one of the few female Cleveland College students who showed an interest in world affairs. Around the end of my first year, still fascinated with the newly established United Nations (UN), I interviewed three religious leaders about it: a Catholic priest, a Rabbi, and another Christian leader. The UN was created with the goal of international peace and harmony, but larger countries were already taking a dominant position over the smaller ones. I asked each of them what they thought about that.

As it turned out, the most memorable part of these interviews was meeting a Catholic priest for the first time; I was very nervous! I got through the interview without an incident and published my article in the June 1946 Cleveland College quarterly literary magazine.

By the second semester, the war was over. The G.I. Bill of Rights had been passed, so men and women who had served were able to go to college for free. (I learned much later that Black soldiers were often unable to take advantage of the bill's benefits.) The influx of young men into the college was wonderful. They had been through so much, seen the world, and knew about much more than the women at the college. Most of the women on campus were not at all politically interested. I just loved the conversations I could have with these worldly men.

Unfortunately, as soon as the war ended, our country

began to experience a strong wave of anti-Communist hysteria. This "Red Scare" made it very difficult to move progressive issues forward, and the college wasn't immune. One day in sociology class, the professor—who was also the Assistant Dean of the college—proclaimed, "I won't fire any professor I suspect of being a Communist until the anti-Communist hysteria dies down, *but then I will.*"

That way his reasoning for firing the professor would be less transparent. Dean John Barden also said that members of the Communist Party had to swear allegiance to the Soviet Union. Someone in the class courageously stood up and said loudly and clearly, "No they don't!" That student was Henry Gluck, a good friend of mine from the Young Progressives.

The Young Progressives was the youth section of the Progressive Party which supported Henry Wallace for President in 1948. A group of us at Cleveland College had formed a local chapter. Wallace ran on a platform of racial desegregation, establishing a national health insurance system, and conciliation with the Soviet Union, among other progressive issues.

When we started, I may have been the only woman in the group. Many of the other members were veterans—they'd seen war and had good reason to work for peace under Wallace. Just to be clear, I didn't choose my activities to show what women can do; but I did what I felt needed to be done and hoped for the best. If I was pushing the boundaries of what was expected for women to do, it was a welcome side effect.

I was just as excited as anyone in the Progressive Party to learn that Wallace would be speaking at a local union conference. Unfortunately, that also meant it would be competitive getting a seat at the event. I didn't know how I would get a ticket but could not imagine missing the chance to see him. I had to get creative. Based on my track record writing for college publications, I convinced the editors of the college newspaper to send me to the meeting to write an article about it. So, I got a press pass!

I entered the large conference room, and it was filled almost entirely with men. When Wallace walked in, everyone got up out of their seats to applaud and cheer! He was then enthusiastically introduced as "the next President of the United States." Before that day, I had no idea so many Wallace supporters were in the area; people who believed in racial equality, desegregation, and an end to the Cold War. It was such an empowering, unifying feeling that it brought tears to my eyes.

The next day I scribbled a short poem in the top margin of a paper I handed in for English Literature: "If a new world you would create, remember it's Wallace in '48."

The teacher was less than impressed. He wrote back, "Verses like this I abominate, no matter who in '48." I loved it! I still remember both verses over 70 years later!

As the presidential campaign continued, a group of us drove from Cleveland to Philadelphia to attend the 1948 Progressive Party Convention. The Progressive Party would nominate Henry Wallace as their candidate for President at the convention. We rode in an old car that was much too small for the six of us, but we were determined to get there— so we sat on each other's laps! It was a long and uncomfortable trip—but also a lot of fun. I was twenty years old and the voting age was twenty-one, but that didn't lessen my enthusiasm at all.

The Chair of the Cleveland delegation raised our spirits and our sense of unity by leading us in song after song! Eventually, he got hoarse, and another delegate led us until he got hoarse too, so I ended up leading many songs throughout the event. We all snake-danced around the convention hall singing, "Iowa, Iowa, that's where the tall corn grows!" over and over. Wallace was of course from Iowa. It was a young convention and a young, short-lived party.

When Wallace spoke at a rally in Cleveland later in his campaign, my friend Karen and I wanted to go—but it was the same evening as our Great Books course at the college.

We had a hard time deciding whether we should skip class. Of course, we ultimately chose to see Wallace. Somehow, we got to see him backstage after the speech. I was a Zionist then, as was Karen, so we brought him a plant representing a tree that was planted in his honor in Israel.

Libby Frank and Karen Stern greeting the Progressive Party Presidential Candidate Henry Wallace in 1948, Cleveland.

When we returned to class, we had to explain to the professor why we'd skipped class. We made up our own words to "Ballad for Americans" and gave it to the professor, Mr. Harris. One of the verses went:

We had a choice
Between two men
One was Harris, one was Hen
We decided there and then
That Wallace we would hear
That Wallace we would cheer [theme music]

"Hen" Wallace lost the 1948 election for president, and the Progressive Party just about died after his loss. Along with Henry Wallace and Strom Thurmond, Republican Thomas Dewey ran for president against Democrat Harry Truman. It was widely predicted Dewey would win. There's a famous photograph of Truman holding up a premature headline saying Dewey *had* won, which was printed before the votes were even counted. I appreciated the irony of that photo.

I researched and wrote a paper about the election: "Why the public opinion polls failed to predict the outcome: Polling the pollsters." My mailbox literally overflowed with explanations from the pollsters. I was amazed at how many of them responded. My mother was less excited about that.

While I was disheartened by the outcome of the election, I was determined to keep working for the progressive goals that made up Wallace's platform. One lost election was not going to defeat our struggle for peace and justice.

I focused my energies on other groups, such as the Labor Youth League. While this group focused on workers' rights, peace, and racial equality, I was disappointed to find that our club had all white members. We kept organizing events to diversify our membership, but it wasn't working. We would announce the location and invite Black youth we knew—and none of them came. We finally realized that people have to be part of the planning, organizing, decision-making, and policymaking in order to feel welcome. That lesson stayed with me into all of my future organizing.

We were always looking to grow the organization, recruiting other like-minded youth to support progressive issues. One time we had a competition between the Detroit and Cleveland LYL (Labor Youth League) clubs for who could recruit the most members to the organization. Whichever club lost the competition had to host the members of the club that won. We were a competitive group, and Cleveland won! I was excited to go to Detroit, but I didn't want my parents to know where I was going. They never knew for sure what groups I belonged to. What if the newspaper did an exposé on our gathering in Detroit and my parents found out why I was there? Instead, I lied and said I was going to New York.

The Labor Youth League did become more racially integrated than most organizations, but some members of our group also did some stupid things. For example, I helped organize a convention in Cleveland that included a dance. At the dance, the white people were dancing with white people and the Black people dancing with Black people. The chair of the League stopped the music and said, "Every white person has to dance with a Negro."

It was awful. I got into several arguments with people about this situation and other backward attitudes. One time, when I shook hands with a local leader, he said I was shaking hands too hard, and it was unbecoming a woman! At a house meeting I attended, someone told me it was unsuitable to sit on the floor, because one day we'd be running the country and we needed to be more dignified. It was frustrating to face these issues within the same organization that was fighting *against* racism and inequality. But I continued with the group, because I knew we were making a difference for workers' rights and desegregation.

Part of advancing workers' rights involved supporting union strikes. In 1949, Don Rothenberg invited me to a strike by the International Association of Machinists (IAM). I knew Don from his role as the chief organizer of the local Young Progressives and we were friends. The union had asked for a show of solidarity from anyone who could make it early in the morning. The timing corresponded to when the shifts changed and "scabs"—protected by the police—would try to enter the factory. Don picked me up at home. I carried my shoes and tiptoed out of my apartment so that my parents wouldn't ask me where I was going. Don drove to the road leading to the factory. Down one side of the road I could see a line of the strikers' cars. All of the strikers were behind their cars, where Don and I joined them.

The leader of the union was a woman named Marie Reed Haug, and her husband, Fred, was a member too. She was very tall and very sure of herself; a good role model during a time when I saw few female leaders. We were all crouched down behind the cars, waiting for the scabs to drive their cars down the road, protected by police on horseback. When they did, Marie stood up and yelled to the strikers, "Come on men!"

All the union men rose and threw marbles under the horses. The horses fell. It was a traumatic experience. When I decided to go, I didn't know what would actually happen to stop the scabs. I understood that the workers called for help, and I went to show solidarity. I learned later that this method was not unique to IAM and many other unions and protestors did the same. Sensitivity to animal welfare was nothing like it is now. They didn't think about it the way we do today.

My later support of unions was more peaceful. I supported a very strong and creative national boycott of non-union grown grapes in the 1960s. The conditions for the farm workers were horrible: limited water, minimal rest, awful housing, child labor, and more. I went with other protestors to a large chain supermarket, and we all filled up our shopping carts with groceries and non-union grapes. When we went to check out, we each asked the cashier if the grapes were produced by union workers. If they said "no," or "we don't know," we left the cart there with all the groceries. The grocery store workers were annoyed, but it made a strong statement.

We also plastered "Don't Buy Non-Union Grapes" stickers on boxes of non-union grapes. We knew it was effective because friends outside were giving leaflets to incoming shoppers and learned that many of them refused to buy the grapes.

I helped copy the leaflets while working part-time at the

Bureau of Jewish Education office. I did miscellaneous tasks, including running off articles and lesson plans on a copy machine. I brought a pile of legitimate papers to copy on the machine but had a copy of the grape boycott leaflet hidden within them. I had just started on my leaflet when I heard my boss, Mr. Levitin, coming down the steps. I quickly hid my leaflets under the school papers and escaped discovery. The scare didn't stop me from making more flyers though.

I also worked with organizations such as the Council of Jewish Women to organize campaigns to close sweatshops and end the horrible conditions overseas. We went to local clothing stores and asked the managers if they knew where and under what conditions the clothes were produced. Then we distributed informational leaflets to educate them. Most people didn't know about the terrible work conditions in other countries. Of course, our own country has a history of textile worker abuse. Upton Sinclair's novel, *The Jungle*, and other exposés helped inspire the labor reforms and worker rights we have today.

When the IAM strike took place, attacks on Communist Party members went hand-in-hand with attacks on unions, especially left-wing ones like the IAM. After the strike failed, many strikers and union workers were arrested, including at least one friend of mine, Norman Berman. He was arrested for "trying to influence the Court" because he wrote a letter to the judge regarding the legal challenges against the union. These trumped-up charges were typical of the time.

•

I tried to keep my parents in the dark about my involvement in political action, but I continued living at home while I went to college. For a long time, my brother and I continued to share a bedroom with twin beds. Some nights we talked with each other in bed before he went to sleep; but not about politics. He would plan to stay awake until I came to bed later and then we talked quietly to avoid detection from our parents. It was a treat for us both. That's when I felt most like the older sister.

During one of these talks, we started working on his bar mitzvah speech. Picture a thirteen-year-old boy standing up in front of dozens of relatives and friends, unfurling a long paper scroll. He began:

> From the book I didn't want a speech
> It wouldn't be sincere, so I have right here—
> But wait, don't go home
>
> I don't have a speech; I just have a poem.
> I thank you all for coming tonight.
> But it really would not be just right
>
> If I didn't say thanks to my friends so fine
> Who worked so hard for the dinner divine.
> The chickens they koshered, the chickens they
>   cooked
>
> If they were caterers, they'd be solidly booked.
> Thanks for the strudel, and all that you've done,
> And now I'll quit, and we'll all have some fun.

We celebrated with a homemade party in the Lakeview Hebrew School auditorium. My mother's friends cooked and we (the women and girls of course) served a sit-down dinner. We didn't have buffets back then! For entertainment, we had a fiddle player and I loved it—it was really *schmaltzy*[1]. We danced and ate and eventually cleaned up. I had invited my friend Noach from high school; it was nice having a platonic boyfriend with me.

My father's father, who we called Zayde, had come in

---

1 Schmaltzy: emotional or sentimental. For me, it was soul music.

from his home in McKeesport and we gave him a watch to celebrate his eighty-third birthday. According to Jewish lore, a person's lifespan is 70 years. That meant Zayde was celebrating his second bar mitzvah! Sadly, my grandmother had died by that time and wasn't around to celebrate this milestone.

This event was one of the last times we were all peaceful together. As I became more involved in peace and justice work, my home life became more difficult—with my parents and even my brother Marvin disapproving of the choices I made.

Soon after I graduated from college, I had to move out. At that time girls didn't leave home unless they were going to college or getting married. I had already graduated from college and was certainly not getting married—my moving out was practically a scandal.

When I was in college, my parents often worried about my progressive activism, especially issues involving "Negroes." One Saturday evening after dinner, I was getting ready to go to a dance and I let slip that it was an interracial dance. My father was desperate to change my mind. He offered to buy me a fur coat if I didn't go. Of all the things I *didn't* want, a fur coat was probably at the top of the list. So bourgeois! If he had offered a trip around the world, I might have considered not going to the dance, but he really didn't know me. I went to the dance.

I met my lifelong friend Mike in the Young Progressives. Her real name was Vivian, but her father wanted a son, so her nickname was Mike. My parents wouldn't let me have Mike come over to our house because she was Black. She only lived two blocks away! Things got really difficult for me at home when Mike was planning her wedding to Carlos. Mike asked me to be maid of honor. I was thrilled to be invited as a member of the wedding party. I'd never been in a wedding before! It was going to be a small affair at her parents' house and Mike's mother was going to sew us dresses. Her grandfather was a preacher and would conduct the ceremony.

Both my parents vehemently opposed my being part of the wedding. My mother had never talked to Mike's mother before, but my mother called her and begged her, "Get Mike to change her mind about having Libby be her maid of honor."

Mike's mother replied: "Mrs. Gisser, I have as much control over my daughter as you have over yours."

It was such a perfect response by Mike's mother. Mike told me about it. After finding out about that call, I felt I had to get out of my parents' home. I moved out shortly before the wedding in order to be Mike's maid of honor. I temporarily stayed in an apartment with Don Rothenberg and his wife, Linda.

In the meantime, my mother actually tried to get me fired. *My own mother!* I was teaching Hebrew school at two different places. My mother first called Rabbi Brickner at the Reform temple where I was teaching and tried to get me fired there. I went to see him about it and as I entered his office, he proclaimed, "Libby, you look wonderful! Did you get engaged?"

I said, "No, I moved out."

I kept that job, but my whole family—including my younger brother—was upset with me for moving out.

My mother also called the principal of the Orthodox Talmud Torah school, Yetta. In addition to being the school principal, Yetta was a friend of my family. (Many years later, after my mother had died, my dad married Yetta.) My mother told Yetta I was going to be in a *Christian* wedding and that I shouldn't teach in a Jewish school anymore. She didn't say it was a "Negro" wedding, yet if Mike were *white* and Christian, it wouldn't have bothered my parents so much. Yetta didn't know what to do. She spoke with another teacher, who happened to be an Israeli young man. He said, "You American-Jews want to be accepted, but if somebody asks you to be in a non-Jewish wedding party, you say no?"

His response convinced Yetta, and my job there was safe as well.

My relationship with my parents was tense for a long time. In the Jewish tradition, one year after burial, the family has a ceremony to unveil the gravestone. I planned to join my family for my grandfather's unveiling ceremony in McKeesport. My parents told me I would be desecrating my grandfather's grave if I participated in the wedding and then attended the unveiling ceremony. Since I knew when they were going, I showed up at my parents' home early that morning. They had nothing to say to me—but they did not stop me from getting in the car with them to drive to McKeesport together.

Eventually my mother and I started talking again. I visited her when my dad was at work. I knew she still didn't approve of my activities and once overheard her say to a friend, "Libby was such a good girl! I don't understand how she got herself involved in these political issues."

My mother was right in some ways. I had mostly been a "good girl" growing up. I tried to do what was expected of me and stay out of trouble. But I had a rebellious streak, too. When I was around six years old, we lived near a field which I had to cross to get from our house to the school. We lived so close that if I started running from the house when I heard the school bell ring, I could still make it to class on time. One week it snowed and then it rained. The snow was melting and created huge puddles in the field. I saw a group of boys happily slopping through the puddles and it looked like so much fun! Even though I had on my good shoes, I jumped in too. I was the only girl who did it. Unfortunately for my mother, that innocent rebellion grew into a habit of challenging the status quo.

My mother's concern about my speaking out also had

deep roots. I still remember very clearly peering over my mother's shoulder to read a 1936 newspaper headline. Ten thousand people had been killed in Ethiopia after Italy invaded the country, under the direction of Benito Mussolini. I gasped aloud, "That's terrible!"

My mother said, "Shh!"

I was eight years old and entirely unaware of the politics, but my mother was well-informed. We were living in an Italian neighborhood, and she was scared of someone overhearing my comment. Her fear was echoed by many Jewish families who came to this country after fleeing oppression in Europe and Tsarist Russia. My mother, Rachel Hocheiser, was born in Austria or Hungary. (The land changed "ownership" so many times through wars and occupations, it's hard to pinpoint which country it was at the time.) Years later, my friends and I talked about our parents "bringing the Tsar with them" when they immigrated to the United States—in their fear of attracting attention. I have struggled against the "Shh!" my whole life, but I couldn't stand what the people in charge did to the rest of us—and that's what drove me to keep speaking out.

Developing a Global Perspective

In 1951, I joined thousands of other peace and justice activists at the third World Youth Festival hosted in East Germany. The festival was organized by the World Federation of Democratic Youth—made up of youth organizations from all over the world. The festival advocated for solidarity, peace, and resistance to war with the motto "For Peace and Friendship—Against Nuclear Weapons." In 1951, those ideas were considered borderline Communist.

This trip was my first of many outside the U.S. and was part of the reason I became a lifelong peace and justice activist. It gave me a global perspective on war, oppression, and creative ways that they were being challenged.

Getting to the conference was my biggest challenge. After WWII, Germany was divided into West Germany, known as the Federal Republic of Germany, and East Germany, known as the German Democratic Republic (GDR). The GDR was not recognized by the Allied countries for many years, so getting there from the United States was a complicated process.

I first had to get a passport. Many young Americans who had planned on attending the festival either couldn't get their passports or had them revoked by the State Department. I was nervous about whether I'd get mine, considering my own affiliations. I also had an issue with my birth certificate which slowed down the process. When I was born, my parents couldn't agree on my name, so the birth certificate only said, "Baby Gisser." I had to get one of my parents to sign notarized papers with my real first name, but I couldn't let them know why. They were already afraid my political activity might cause me to be targeted; they would never cooperate if they knew where I was going. Somehow, I got my dad to sign the form without him pushing for details. Luckily, the birth certificate papers helped me successfully get my passport. I celebrated when I received it!

I also needed to raise enough money to afford the trip. During WWII, the U.S. government sold war bonds for $18.75 apiece for the war effort. After 10 years you could cash them in for $25. I had a few saved up and cashed those in, ironically, to help pay for my trip. I contacted supporters in the progressive movement and asked for donations to help fund the rest of the trip.

By this time, I had moved out of Don Rothenberg's place into a third-floor attic apartment. It was a private home owned by a very friendly Jewish family. Some months later, I got a call from a New York friend about a young woman named Miriam (Mimi) Schwartz. Mimi was moving from New York to Cleveland to attend graduate school for social work and she needed a place to live.

Our apartment was one bedroom with two beds, a kitchen, living room, bathroom, and a small, somewhat rickety balcony off the living room. We took our chances and slept out there on hot nights to escape the heat of the apartment—air conditioning was a luxury back then that we weren't wealthy enough to afford.

Mimi was around my age and a progressive activist as well. During our six years there, Mimi and I became good friends and comrades in our activist work. While I was at the festival, Mimi wired me funds from my supporters several times when I ran out of money. Without my involvement in progressive organizations and the supporters who believed in the importance of a global movement, I would not have been able to go.

Our journey began on a Cunard ship sailing from New York to France. I took a train from Cleveland to New York and stayed with my Aunt Anna and Uncle Sam. The next morning, Aunt Anna accompanied me to the pier, never knowing that I was on my way to the World Youth Festival. I was very excited—but I didn't know *anyone* on the ship yet. The travel agent had told me how many people on the ship were going to the festival, but she couldn't tell me their names for safety reasons.

As we were sailing away, I stood on the deck with many of the passengers and heard someone on the dock yell to the young man standing next to me, "If you get to Italy kiss the pope's left foot for me!"

I laughed picturing this large man bending over to kiss the foot of the statue of Saint Peter. He is considered the first pope and is honored with a statue in Vatican City. Touching the toe of Saint Peter is said to bring good luck. I had a feeling this young man was also headed to the festival. I talked to him and found out I was right. He introduced himself as Stan, and because he was so tall, we all called him "Big Stan."

Next I met Doris Mallard—one of very few non-whites on the ship—who was also going to the festival. She was in a private room by herself because they wouldn't room her with any of the white passengers. We were both traveling third class, of course—it was the cheapest way to go—but somehow, I was assigned to a room with women who had big corsages and fancy clothes; very bourgeois. I wasn't at all comfortable with them. Doris had two bunkbeds in her room and she agreed to let me move in with her. When we went to the bursar to let him know about the room change, he said he couldn't let us do that. Not to be deterred, Doris and I stood our ground and threatened to sue for racial discrimination. Minutes later, I moved in with Doris. It felt good to achieve this small victory on our way to a festival for solidarity and peace.

After landing in France, our group took a train to Paris, where we stayed in a nice, small hotel called the Quirinal. I'd taken French in high school and stayed up all night practicing my French with the night clerk.

France was also an Allied country and wouldn't let us travel from Paris to East Berlin, so we took another train to a coastal town in France. We were supposed to pretend we were ordinary tourists and not going to the Youth Festival, but we heard a rumor that the train car behind us had a group of French people also going to the festival. My new friend Doris and I decided to go back there to meet the young French people. As soon as they saw us, they knew we were going to the festival as well; she was Black, I was white, and we were young—it couldn't have been more obvious.

They asked us to sing "Joe Hill," an American political song. Joe Hill organized workers through the Industrial Workers of the World and wrote political songs and poems. He was executed in 1915 on a murder charge that many considered to be a frame-up. We sang it for them.

Then they asked, "What would you like us to sing?" We didn't know any French songs except Frère Jacques, which was very embarrassing for us. They knew "Joe Hill," a radical working-class song and all we knew was a French nursery rhyme. We all had a good laugh about it and then continued talking about our different experiences.

When we arrived in the French coastal town, we saw another train full of young people from the U.K. Hundreds of them were hanging out of the train windows with flags and banners! The rest of the world had heard about the State Department limiting American travelers, so they were especially excited when we showed up. They cheered and clapped and called us brave. Danny Rubin, one of the U.S. delegation leaders, had an American flag hidden inside the lining of his jacket. As we headed to the boat, Danny removed the flag and waved it at the cheering crowd. We spaced ourselves out as we walked so it would look like there were more of us. It was astonishing and thrilling to be applauded by the others—we were all used to being harassed at home and here they were celebrating our attendance.

Youth from the U.S., France, and the United Kingdom all headed to the Polish ship, "The Batory," that was scheduled to take us to Germany. After we boarded the ship, we had a wonderful celebration singing together and dancing in circles.

"Maintenant il commence!" one of the French people said. "Now, it begins."

It was my first experience with young people from other countries and it gave me a taste of what we'd soon be experiencing at the festival.

Libby Frank with joyous young people on the way to the World Youth Festival in 1951, The Batory.

Germany had been destroyed from Allied bombing during WWII and it was very slowly recovering. Air raid shelters still dotted the city, many collapsed and forgotten, with destruction all around. We were hosted in a school in East Berlin. Every morning our hosts gave us a hard-boiled egg, an orange, coffee, and bread for breakfast. It was luxurious compared to what most Germans had at the time. We noticed a few Germans looking in the window—whether out of hunger or curiosity we didn't know—but we felt guilty. Very few Germans had the luxury of real coffee, eggs, or oranges. We told our generous East German hosts we would have only bread and coffee and asked them to give the rest of the meal to the nearby residents.

During the day, we attended workshops to learn about ways to advance peace. We also heard reports from representatives of each country that attended—including capitalist, socialist, and developing countries. In the evening, groups from different countries performed for everyone. The U.S. delegates didn't know each other beforehand, so we didn't have a group to perform, but we had some talented individual performers. Hope Foye was a wonderful African American singer, and she got on stage to sing "Strange Fruit":

> Southern trees bear strange fruit
> Blood on the leaves and blood on the root

Doris and I were backstage during Hope's performance. It was very difficult for Doris because her father had been hanged for organizing voters in the South. I could not imagine how awful it must have been for her. We were determined to bring home new ideas from the festival to end this kind of violence.

The festival welcomed people of all backgrounds and colors, but my friend Doris wanted to know what it was like beyond the festival grounds. The only Black people the Germans had previously seen were Black soldiers who had helped liberate Germany. Doris wanted to walk around East Berlin to see how people treated her. One day we left the grounds to explore the city.

We came to a produce store where we saw a small wood statue of a "pickaninny" out front. This common stereotype of a Black boy eating watermelon with a big grin and a sunhat bothered both of us, but especially Doris. A policeman happened to pass by and Doris—without her knowing any German or the policeman knowing English—indicated her discomfort with the statue. To our great surprise, the policeman went into the shop and the owner came out to remove the statue!

I learned later that the GDR was very strict about who could serve in the justice department (from police officer to judge) or in education (from pre-school to university). To serve in these roles, people had to either be Jewish, have served in the war against the Nazis, or have been out of the country during the war. This might have explained the policeman's sensitivity to Doris' discomfort. This side of the GDR was never represented by the U.S. media. Instead, the GDR was vilified because of its ties to the Communist Soviet Union. I experienced firsthand the stark difference between what the media portrayed and the reality of interacting directly with people. It would not be the last time I had that experience.

In addition to the workshops and performances, my favorite part of the festival was all the singing. The last night of the festival, thousands of us snake-danced through the streets, singing the World Youth Song in different languages. Fireworks were going off. It was absolutely electrifying to be a part of that moment. Participating in the World Youth Festival solidified my commitment to *global* peace and justice. Considering different perspectives was unpopular—from McCarthyism to the Cold War to the Middle East conflicts— but that's what is needed to bridge international divides and discover common goals. Recognizing the similarities between all of our struggles, and learning from each other, gave us renewed purpose and new insights to take home to our respective countries.

After the festival, I had plans to visit a friend who had moved to Israel. I decided to make a stop in London to visit "Little Stan" from the Cunard ship. Little Stan was one of two young maritime workers from London who had jumped ship when they arrived in New York. They were caught and sent back on the Cunard ship, but they had to live in the hold, the basement of the ship. Little Stan and the other maritime worker, Eric, had raw rum in their room, which they brought up to our room for nightly parties with them and others who were going to the festival.

I had planned to meet with Little Stan in London. How to get there? We couldn't go by land through West Germany to get a flight to England, so I left Berlin by boat with some other festival attendees. When I arrived at the London airport, the authorities asked me to declare how much money I had with me. Even though I had wired home to Mimi a couple times for more money—which she forwarded from supporters—I only had $10 left after the festival. When I admitted this to the airport authorities, they didn't want to let me into the country. Luckily, Little Stan, a British citizen, was there to meet me and the authorities let me enter England. They didn't know he also had only $10! I stayed with Stan's family and they were very welcoming.

My next stop was Israel. I had a plan to fly from London to Naples, where I would take a boat to Haifa. I had two pieces of luggage and my purse. On the train down to Naples, I couldn't fit all of my luggage in my compartment. I had to leave one suitcase in the public passageway, and it was stolen during the trip. People in my compartment were very upset the theft had happened in Italy—their country.

I was traveling third class on the train, trying to make each part of the trip as inexpensive as possible. I didn't realize women didn't travel alone in third class at the time, so I was the only unescorted woman in the car. Three young Italian men in the car came over to talk to me. Through broken English and Italian, the men said we'd be arriving in Naples at midnight and asked where I would stay until morning. I said I couldn't stay in a hotel because I had only enough money to stay two nights until my boat left for Israel. I had planned on staying in the train station until it got light. Their faces suggested I had an unrealistic idea of what the station would be like. When we got off at Naples, one of the men accompanied me to a little café in the station and stayed with me. After I ate, I put my head down on the table and slept while he stayed awake to protect me. We parted ways in the morning, and I didn't realize until after he was gone that he had put money in my pocket. I was so touched to have this stranger looking out for me. It was one of several experiences that showed me how generous and helpful people can be.

I set off in search of a cheap, safe hotel and I found a policeman who spoke some English. He took me to one hotel after another. At each hotel he asked if I would be safe; specifically if they would keep male visitors out of my room. One after another, they all said no. With all the walking around we did, it was actually a relief to not have both of my suitcases. We finally came to a small hotel where the owner said he could keep me safe and keep people out of my room. I checked in there and was ready to explore the city.

This kind policeman took me under his wing. He bought me pizza for breakfast, then he stopped at a shoe store and got me a pair of sandals because mine were in the stolen suitcase. He showed me the city of Naples and took me back to the hotel when it got dark. Amusingly, the policeman wanted to come up to the room and the manager wouldn't let him! The next day the policeman had to be on duty, and he had a friend take me around the city again.

Then it was time to sail from Naples to Haifa. The Israeli

sailors aboard were very attentive because most of the people on the ship were older. I was staying in a huge room with a bunch of women and children who were seasick and throwing up. It was awful. The Israeli sailors took pity on me and let me eat with them. They let me sleep on deck and took turns keeping watch over me all night. The sunsets and the sunrises were stunning over the Mediterranean. It was wonderful.

On the boat, I met up with a group of teenage Jewish boys from Algeria who were going to live in Israel. I spoke French with them and Hebrew with the sailors; and at night, I dreamed in those languages. It was the first and only time I've ever dreamed in another language. I didn't speak English for two days.

One of the Israeli sailors was going to show me around Haifa after we landed. I was to wait for him until he finished his chores on board the ship. However, when I arrived on shore in Haifa, I was surprised to hear someone call my name!

Joe Schwartz had been a good friend in Cleveland but had moved to live on a kibbutz[1] in Israel. I was surprised and delighted to see him. I asked, "How did you know I was here?"

Joe said he heard someone at his kibbutz talking about the World Youth Festival and he asked if anyone from Cleveland attended. The person told him, "Yes, Libby Gisser! And she's coming here."

Joe was thrilled to hear my name and he decided to show me around Israel. I felt bad ditching the Israeli sailor, but of course I went with Joe. Back then, you could hitchhike through the city. The bus system barely existed. It was a

---

1 A kibbutz was a cooperative group of people who lived and worked together, often as farmers.

developing country. After spending the day with Joe, I went to visit my friend, Natan, at Kibbutz Barcai.

On his kibbutz, couples lived together without being married; it was shocking. Once a year, a rabbi came around and made a marriage ceremony for all of them followed by dancing and celebration. I spent only twenty-four hours on the kibbutz with Natan before it was time to board the ship to go home.

On the way back to New York, the ship made a stop in Greece to see the Acropolis. I didn't have any money left for a ticket, but someone on the ship paid my way. I was amazed at the kindness of strangers throughout my trip.

When we arrived back in New York, many passengers were exclaiming, "Finally, American coffee!" I had never drunk coffee before but that's when I started, and I haven't stopped since.

As I was preparing to disembark, an official on the ship called my name. I was terrified that the State Department had found out I went to the GDR and that they were going to take my passport. Instead, it was a telegram from Mimi. She had sent money for me to get home by train. It was such a relief!

The Power of Folk Music

One of the groups I joined after college was a young integrated group called Folkcul, an abbreviated reference to folk culture. Most of our actions focused on challenging Jim Crow laws. We planned picnics at public swimming pools that didn't allow Black people. White and Black, we'd all go into the pool together. We would take a bus to the action and sing together the whole way. It made us feel connected and powerful—even if sometimes all we sang was "100 Bottles of Beer on the Wall."

Singing has been a stream running through all I've done. Whether it was singing with Folkcul on our bus trips, the World Youth Festival, folk concerts, or just in people's homes (known as hootenannies), music acted as a powerful tool for inspiring action. I felt a sense of solidarity and community when singing with other activists—freedom songs, labor songs, silly songs, revolutionary songs, or foreign-language songs. Groups of us got together, usually accompanied by guitars and banjos. As a friend of mine wrote: *A song reaches us on a level intellect alone can't.* When we sang loudly and robustly, we could feel the whole house shaking. It felt like our music was defying everything bad, and together we could change the world.

At the time, as it still is now, certain cops were assigned

to spy on progressive activities. They were known as The Red Squad. We had picket lines and chanted about the Red Squad—who were often watching us. One time during a pool integration action, we saw a camera sticking out of a window of the pool house taking pictures of what we were doing. No face showed; the window shade was pulled down on top of the camera. We were sure it was the Red Squad. One of us—it might have been me—took a picture of the camera in the window to show we weren't scared. Actually, we were scared, but we could not let them intimidate us.

Another time we went to a segregated pool in Youngstown, Ohio. Not only did we get kicked out of the pool, but we were warned never to come back to Youngstown again! We also visited a pool in Cleveland with the NAACP Youth Group. I worked with wonderful people in Folkcul and some of them became good friends.

One evening a few of us, white and Black, went to a small bar to relax and hear the local band perform. We were sitting at a table in the lightly attended space, sipping beer. A band member came up to us and asked who we were. Black and white young people socializing together was very unusual in those days. We didn't identify ourselves as Communists—because most of us weren't—but the band played "The Volga Boatman" in our honor, a popular song from the Soviet Union. The band members were not antagonistic; they just assumed we were Communists. They thought, "Who else relaxed together, regardless of race, in the 1950s?"

On the way to a segregated pool in 1952,
Youngstown or Cleveland, Ohio.

•

Paul Robeson—an African American actor, singer, and activist—was a prominent figure and strong supporter of peace and justice. He and his wife were both thought to be Communists, though he never explicitly confirmed nor denied it. Robeson visited the Soviet Union and surprised everyone when he returned by saying that while he was there, he felt free for the first time. Similar to when Doris and I were in East Germany, he did not experience any racism in the Soviet Union.

Because of his radical politics, Robeson was the victim of many attacks—sometimes physical, sometimes by the government (who took away his passport), and sometimes by the media. Robeson was scheduled to sing at an outdoor concert in Peekskill, New York in 1949. It was a benefit for the Civil Rights Congress. I couldn't attend this event but reading about it and hearing a song about it had a powerful effect on me. He never got to sing at this New York concert. On his way to the event, he was attacked by locals. They threw stones at him and at the cars of the people going to the concert. The worst part was that the police were protecting the stone-throwers. Robeson bravely hosted a second concert the next month and 2,500 trade unionists attended to protect him. Despite their support, concertgoers were again attacked, although not until after the concert.

Later that year, Mimi and I took the trolley to see Paul Robeson sing in Cleveland. As we got closer to the music hall, more and more people, mostly Black, got on the trolley. Almost all of them were going to the concert. It was so exciting. I remember feeling such solidarity with the people on the trolley as it continued to fill up. When we arrived, the music hall was almost completely full. A lot of cops were outside, and we had to navigate our way past them to get into the hall. The Korean War (1950-1953) was threatening to break out and the warm-up act, Martha Schlamme, included an anti-war song in her set.

Martha was a progressive Jewish folk singer who most often sang Yiddish folk songs. This time she sang, "Johnny I Hardly Knew Ye," about a young man who went to war and was barely recognizable on his return, because of what the war did to him. (If you haven't heard it before, you may recognize the tune from a children's song which came out decades later, "The Ants Go Marching.")

> They're rolling out the guns again, harroo, harroo,
> They're rolling out the guns again, harroo, harroo.
> They're rolling out the guns again,

But they never will take our sons again.
No, they never will take our sons again. JOHNNY,
   I SWEAR IT TO YE!"

Every last one of us stood and clapped, stamped our feet, and cheered. It felt like the building shook. The cops came rushing in with their guns drawn. They thought something threatening had happened. Maybe it had. Paul Robeson took the stage next and performed an amazing concert, though it was one of his last. He lived in Philadelphia until his death in 1976; the Paul Robeson House in West Philadelphia is now a nationally recognized historic site and museum.

•

It was a hysterical time in America; it was anti-left, anti-union, anti-peace-and-justice activists, and anti-Communist. Eventually, I was smeared on a series of front pages of the *Cleveland Press* along with other members of Folkcul. A young woman had been attending our meetings for a few months, but it turned out she was actually an undercover reporter. In her articles, she claimed to have seen the "use of a legitimate picnic as a base for a Communist scheme to incite violence," among many other accusations. Violence was never part of our program. A bunch of us were accused of being Communists—some of us were. I was described as a "perennial participant in Communist-backed groups, a delegate to the Youth Festival staged by the Russian Communists in Berlin in August 1951."

A local president of a Protestant youth group said I'd solicited him to join in a project, writing a letter to show Cleveland's goodwill and support for Harrison Dillard, track star from Cleveland, who was in Europe with the American Olympic team at the time. The youth group president dubbed me a Communist and went further saying, "I asked her who was sponsoring the letter and she said the American Youth

Peace Crusade. The idea of such a letter seemed to be good. On checking, I found that the American Peace Crusade was labeled as a subversive organization . . . The incident showed me how these people use a noble event like the Olympic games and a fine man like Dillard to trap the unsuspecting into following a party line[1]."

The party being referenced was of course the Communist Party. Despite not being a Communist group, the American Peace Crusade was considered radical, so even the act of sending a card from young people to our Cleveland representative in the Olympics was suspicious. Another charge of following the Party line was our attempt to integrate public swimming pools in Cleveland and Youngstown. *Communists Use Picnic to Incite Race Riot* (The Cleveland Press, 11/25/52).[2] was boldly written in our local paper. The peace group, Folkcul, was mentioned by name alongside a list of the known members. This article was only one in a long series the paper ran, called "The Red Trap for Youth," which accused our group of using people's support of desegregation and equality to lure them in before turning them into Communists. By portraying Communists as the enemy and suggesting our group was a front for Communism, they undermined support for swimming pool integration and other peace and justice work. In those days, being accused of Communist ideas was enough to be viewed as disloyal and potentially dangerous. No evidence was necessary.

As a result of those articles, I lost my job at a small mailing house. I knew the risks of working on these issues, but I was still surprised and frustrated at the betrayal.

I spent a long time grappling with whether I wanted this book to include my membership in the Communist Party.

---

1   Cleveland College Life, Press Brands CC Political Group as Commie Front, Dec. 8, 1952.
2   The Cleveland Press, Red Trap for Youth, Nov. 25, 1952.

Considering the activist work I did, this may not come as a shock to many of you. The media often portrayed liberal groups like Folkcul as Communist-affiliated, but it was mostly scare tactics. I didn't actually join the Communist Party until later.

My affiliation started after the Progressive Party collapsed. I came to realize that the Labor Youth League was basically a young Communist group. Because of my peace and justice interests, I was invited to join the American Communist Party (CPUSA), which organized activities for peace, racial desegregation, and workers' rights. When I joined, I had such a romantic and idealistic view of the Communist Party. I was surprised and honored to be asked to join such an eminent organization.

It was a dangerous time to be a Communist—or any kind of liberal activist—but that is where much of the courageous action and progressive movements were born, so it was where I needed to be. My political activities for many years were with comrades who viewed the world the same way I did. Over time, I became impatient with the top-down decision-making of the Party. I eventually left, but many of these "Communist" ideas inspired me in later years: the camaraderie; the focus on underlying problems in society; and the importance of being in solidarity with other people.

Besides working for peace, racial desegregation, and workers' rights, I was also drawn to the Communist Party because they were anti-fascist. I was already against the German Nazis and the Italian fascists who worked with them; then I learned about the Spanish Civil War.

In 1931, Spain elected an anti-monarchist secular democratic government that was immediately attacked by Spanish fascists. The newly elected Spanish government asked for help from the U.S. and other Western countries, but they didn't receive it. When I first learned about the war, I knew which side I was on, but I didn't yet have a developed political analysis. It was hard to take it all in. The fact that my government didn't help upset me.

The people defending their country against the fascists were called Loyalists. The well-known author, Ernest Hemingway, covered the war as a journalist on the side of the Loyalists. While no country formally provided military support to the newly elected government, the International Brigades were formed by progressives from all over the world who made their way to Spain to fight alongside the Loyalists.

A group from the U.S., both men and women, took part in the struggle and was known as the Abraham Lincoln Brigade. It was an integrated military force; possibly the first time a Black American officer had command over white troops. The Abraham Lincoln Brigade was a diverse group, made up of workers, professors, teachers, carpenters, and more. The women who joined were mostly nurses and drivers. I read thrilling stories of volunteers who had gone, and I was inspired by these young Americans risking their lives for a cause they believed was righteous.

Tragically, the Loyalists lost. The International Brigades suffered a horrific number of deaths among the volunteers. Ultimately, the volunteers left at the request of the Loyalists because it was clear they couldn't do any more good. The fascists were winning, and it was dangerous to stay. At a farewell parade that the Spanish Loyalists held in their honor, Dolores Ibarruri, a courageous Loyalist leader, gave a speech with the famous line, "We'd rather die than live on our knees . . ." Then the International Brigades completed an emotional and organized withdrawal from Spain. Some say if the fascists had been defeated in Spain, we might never have had WWII. It's sad to consider what could have happened differently.

My husband and I went to Spain in April 1999 for two weeks to see some of the battlefields and explore the magnificent art and music from the war. The Abraham Lincoln Brigades sang songs during the war to keep their spirits up.

Years later, a popular saying was: "We lost the war, but we had better songs." It was true and I have the vinyl records to prove it.

We knew about Jarama Valley from the songs and wanted to learn more. Two contacts we had made through comrades from home met us with their Jeep to take us around and explain what happened. We met Spanish Loyalists who told us why they fought and shared war stories. It was an incredible experience.

I found out that the Communist Party in the U.S. had been instrumental in inspiring and organizing these volunteers. Steve Nelson was a Party leader and one of the Abraham Lincoln Brigade volunteers. I read his book, *The Volunteers*, which described his experiences during the Spanish Civil War.

When Steve Nelson spoke in Cleveland, I went to hear him. A mob of right-wing men gathered outside the event to protest. As people arrived by bus, many elderly, several of us young ones went out to accompany them through the protesters. It was scary.

Once everyone was safely inside, we couldn't hear each other because of the right-wing men shouting outside. I don't know how it happened, but at some point we all stood up and sang the Star-Spangled Banner as loudly as we could. In that moment, we were showing that we were Americans, too. It may have been the only time I felt good singing the national anthem as an adult. The mob outside eventually left and Nelson gave his report.

It was also through the Communist Party that I learned about the World Youth Festival. There's no doubt the international Communist movement supported the festivals and may likely have initiated them. I booked my trip through a New York travel agency run by my comrade, Fay Aptheker. When I had to raise money to afford the trip, several friends contributed. We agreed that I would send reports to Mimi, who would copy and send them to the donors.

Soon after returning from the festival, I saw news headlines that made me feel like getting back on the ship and leaving the U.S. again. The National Party Chairman, Gus Hall, and other leading Communists had been arrested. Gus happened to live in Cleveland, so while he was in jail, I babysat their kids when his wife Elizabeth went to meetings. She often read me the letters Gus sent from jail, which were very moving.

I never learned the Halls' home address, even though I visited their house weekly. I didn't look at the house number or the street name, instead remembering the details of the houses to find my way. No one told me not to learn the address; I just figured it was safer not to know. Most of us didn't even know each other's last names for fear of being forced to reveal information about comrades. It may sound farfetched, but the fear was always present. One day, after I had been babysitting for a while, Elizabeth changed the curtains, and I walked right by—I didn't even recognize the house!

Gus Hall remained in jail for over five years, but eventually he was released and continued his activities leading the CPUSA.

One of the worst examples of anti-Communist hysteria was the execution of Ethel and Julius Rosenberg. In 1953, I read the announcement that they were to be executed; accused of being spies for the Soviet Union. When I learned the Supreme Court would hear their case, I was hopeful. I went with The Cleveland Labor Youth League to Washington, D.C. to demonstrate outside of the White House and try to stop their executions.

We were part of a worldwide movement to save the Rosenberg's lives. We tried our best to prevent their execution. We went out on the street with leaflets to encourage others to protest. Most people did not respond well. They yelled at me, closed their windows, ignored me, or called me a Communist. I don't remember ever feeling as angry and desperate about any issue.

My parents knew that I was protesting their execution and my father would not even talk to me about it. My mother said, "I can understand, but why does it have to be *you?*" As always, she was afraid I might be targeted for my activism. I didn't answer, but I knew why: *if not me, then who?*

Despite the best efforts of people around the world, the Rosenbergs were executed, and the news was broadcast across the country. Our best efforts were not good enough. At home, Mimi and I listened to the live broadcast. For years after, I thought I'd actually been outside of the White House on the day the Rosenbergs were executed. My memory of the moment was so clear; but I later confirmed with Mimi that I had just been listening with such intensity that it felt like I was there.

I was devastated by the outcome. I still believe the killing of the Rosenbergs was a put-up job that was due partly to anti-Semitism and partly to the anti-Communist hysteria. They were parents of two young children, and they were denied their right to life. It was incredibly unfair.

The execution of the Rosenbergs had a lasting impact. In the early 1960s, I was living in Columbus, Ohio, when a letter to the Editor appeared in the *Columbus Dispatch*, the major daily. It threatened a member of the local Women for Peace group whose last name was Rosenberg. It said, "Remember what happened to the Rosenbergs," in reference to Julius and Ethel Rosenberg.

One morning our local Rosenberg family woke up to find feces all over the front of their house. It was awful. For several nights, friends stayed at their house overnight to keep watch. My husband took a shift. Nothing happened after the first incident, but the Rosenbergs were understandably shaken.

As in previous situations, accusations of Communism

were used as a way to undermine people involved in peace and justice work.

•

Part of our work with the Communist Party involved accepting work assignments. Along with another young comrade, I was assigned to join the young adults group of the local Jewish Community Center. Our goal was to move them ahead on progressive issues through open discussions. We were always careful not to expose ourselves as Party members. Before leaving for the community center, our local Communist leader warned us not to sing any songs that might expose us. I remember him saying, "The Hammer song's a give-away. Don't sing the Hammer song."

One evening after playing ping pong at the community center, everybody got to singing. Someone in the group asked, "Do you know the Hammer song?" My comrade and I worked to keep the amusement off our faces—so much for the warning! We all sang along together:

> It's the song about love
> Between all of my brothers
> All over this land

The lyrics hadn't been changed to include "my sisters" yet.

We enjoyed engaging with these young, open-minded people. Later, my assignment was changed to working with young teenagers, mostly the children of Party members. I tried and it was a fiasco. At our first meeting, I gave them copies of the Communist Manifesto and told them to read it and come back with questions. Hah! It didn't work out well. I kept trying but didn't have much enthusiasm for it and left that assignment before long. But we had a good time with the first assignment, talking with people our own age about things we all felt were important.

•

From my first folk concert I realized the power of singing together. I was in college and my friend Karen told me about a concert just outside of Cleveland. We went and I was absolutely blown away. It was deeply emotional. That concert got me hooked on folk music and progressive action. American folk singer and political activist, Ronnie Gilbert, said it well: "We felt if we sang loud enough and strong enough and hopefully enough, somehow it would make a difference.[3]"

For a few years in Cleveland, I was part of an informal singing group called the Friendship Chorus. We were a local group, but we also had visiting singers like Woody Guthrie and Pete Seeger. These wonderful performers couldn't sing in any public place because they were considered too radical to hire.

Pete Seeger was a hero of mine from way, way back. His politically themed folk music was part of what got me interested in the progressive movement. Whenever Seeger was in Cleveland, I made sure to see him. One time it was a children's concert, meaning you had to bring a child to attend. Unmarried and childless at the time, I borrowed my friend Mike's son Jimmy to get into the concert.

For our Friendship Chorus, I learned to play enough guitar to get people singing. My friend Blanche Livingstone gave me the guitar as a gift because I babysat her kids one New Year's Eve. If I played a few notes, people were encouraged to sing and they never even noticed when I stopped playing. I didn't know how to play an entire song, but I was good at getting people singing.

____

3 Lieberman, Robbie. My Song is My Weapon: People's Songs, American Communism, and the Politics of Culture, 1995.

In 1951, our singing group was set to perform at a Progressive Party rally where Seeger would sing. That morning we were sitting on the floor in the theater lobby where he came to teach us some songs. One of them was the Hammer song. The chorus at the time was, "I'd sing about love between all my brothers, all over this land."

And I said, "Why just my brothers?"

Maybe 40 years later, I was asked to speak at a large rally in New York to raise money for a Protestant minister accused of taking money from the Soviet Union and not reporting it. He was in danger of being jailed and we were raising money for a defense lawyer. Seeger was going to perform.

Everyone who was part of the program met up in a room beforehand, and I finally got to approach Seeger after all those years. Keep in mind I was in awe of him and still am. I said, "Mr. Seeger, my name is Libby Frank and I remember you came to Cleveland and taught us the Hammer song."

He said, "Yes, it was the Friendship Chorus." He remembered the name of our group!

I said, "Mr. Seeger, I remember I asked, 'Why just my brothers?'"

And then he said, "That was you? That's when we changed it! I went and talked to Lee Hayes [another folk musician], and said to Lee, 'We need to change it.' Lee suggested, 'All my siblings' but it didn't work and then we changed it to 'my brothers and my sisters!'"

Then Seeger told the story in front of the entire assemblage. It was very exciting! My friend Ruth Sillman was in the audience, and she yelled "That's our Libby!"

By the time Pete Seeger sang at this fundraiser, I was no longer a member of the Communist Party. In the 1980s a large number of us left the Communist Party, including my husband, friends, and Herbert Aptheker, one of the Party leaders. He was a brilliant man. I took classes with him at the Jefferson School of Social Science. His leaving was a shock to the Party. Those of us who left formed a new organization, the Committees of Correspondence (COC).

The COC was made up of people from a variety of leftist and socialist organizations. It still exists, but we had to change the name because it turned out that a right-wing group in the south had the same name! We changed the name to Committee of Correspondence for Democracy and Socialism (CCDS). My husband and I are still members. Years later, Pete Seeger, Ruby Dee, and Ossie Davis—all progressive activists—sent out a fundraising letter for CCDS.

When I learned through the folk music grapevine that Seeger was going to be in Philadelphia—where we then lived—some members of the local CCDS branch said, "Maybe you can get him to do a concert for us, since he already supports us."

I told them I didn't have the nerve to approach him. But then Seeger sent me a copy of the book, *Where Have All the Flowers Gone*, which is a compilation of a lot of music he's done. In it, he'd written the story of how the song, "If I Had a Hammer" changed because of this "young radical, Libby Frank."

Inside the book was a postcard with one of his signature banjo pictures, which he always drew alongside his autograph. He wrote, "I'll be visiting Philadelphia soon, may I call you?" May Pete Seeger call *me*? Ha!

I had the nerve to call him then. Toshi, his wife, answered the phone and I asked for him. He was 75 or 80 at the time. She said, "He's out back chopping wood and he'll call you back."

He did! I asked if he would do a concert for the CCDS. He said he was only available one morning, so I asked if he would do a breakfast concert for us that one morning, and he agreed. My husband and I arranged to pick him up where he was staying at someone's house in West Philadelphia. I really couldn't believe it. I was going to pick up Pete Seeger in our car, and I was going to introduce him! I stayed awake all night, my mind buzzing as I considered what to say when I introduced him.

I told my colleague David Zackon beforehand, "I have so much to say about what he and his music meant to me and my family. I don't know how I am going to introduce him!"

And David said, "No one is coming to hear your introduction, Libby."

He was right. So I said, "Here's Pete Seeger. No one is here to hear me introduce him."

As a side note, when my husband and I picked Pete up, Mort mentioned that I was still Libby Gisser back when I asked, "Why just my brothers?" Pete promised to update it for future publications. Recently I ordered a copy of the book for a girl I was mentoring for her Bat Mitzvah and sure enough, it said Libby Gisser!

Pete Seeger was an inspiration. His folk music brought people together to work for peace and justice, along with folk singers such as Woody Guthrie, Phil Ochs, Lee Hays, Joan Baez, Holly Near, and others. Folk music was an important part of building support for progressive issues. The fact that folk groups were surveilled and attacked by the federal government shows that we were having an impact.

Part 2

Zionist to Peace Delegate

A People Without a Land

From the 1940s to 1960s it was fairly common for Jewish social activists to be part of the Zionist movement. We had all learned about the Nazi atrocities and genocide starting in the 1930s. We heard about Jewish refugees on rickety boats trying to escape to Palestine before, during, and after the war. Being a Zionist meant that I wanted Israel to provide a refuge for Jews. I even imagined going to live in Israel myself because I believed—along with many others—that it was the only place Jews could be safe. I wanted to help build a free society in Palestine.

When my high school teacher, Mr. Thomas, asked us to write about our ideal community, I based mine on a kibbutz (it included a water tower). By the way, this was the same Mr. Thomas who said my philosophy of life, which included leaving the world better than I found it, was "a load of baloney." The first kibbutz was founded in Palestine in 1909 but the kibbutz movement was at its height in the 1940s while I was in high school.

When Mr. Thomas read my essay, he said, "Nobody uses water towers anymore!" And *that* was baloney because people still use water towers.

I had one outspoken ally in class, who went by his Hebrew name, Noach (his English name was Norman). He was smart.

He would do other subject's homework in the class while Mr. Thomas was teaching. Mr. Thomas would notice him working on something else and say, "Noach, please explain what I told the class."

He would be able to do it perfectly and the whole class loved it.

Noach was also an active Zionist and was preparing to move to Palestine. This was before Israel was a state since Britain had the mandate over Palestine until 1948. At the time all I understood Zionism to mean was that Jewish refugees should have a safe place to go and the place had to be Palestine. My thinking about Palestine has changed drastically.

As a Zionist, I had an idealistic picture in my mind of young, open-shirted Chalutzim (Jewish pioneers) taming the land and populating it. Along with many others, I was taught it was "a land without people for a people without a land." I later realized that a free society had to include the Arabs who lived there. As my thinking evolved over the years, I came to realize that in order for Jews to be safe in Israel, Jews had to be safe everywhere—and Jews could not be safe until *everyone* was safe. This belief became a foundation of my post-Zionist activity, but it was a gradual development, and it would be several years before I reached this conclusion.

•

My parents were observant Jews. My father was especially observant, but my mother cooperated. Henry Gisser, my father, was born in Galicia, Poland along with four siblings. He celebrated his birthday every year according to the Hebrew lunar calendar, and it usually came around the end of the year, but sometimes it was the beginning of the year. For that reason, some years he would have two birthdays and other years he wouldn't have any. Finally, we told him,

"You have to pick a day to celebrate your birthday on *our* calendar."

And my cheeky Jewish observant father said, "Okay, December 25. If it was good enough for Jesus, it's good enough for me!"

My parents kept a kosher home. We shopped at Jewish-owned grocery stores and bakeries. Often on Sunday mornings, I'd walk with my father to the corner deli and buy white fish and chubs and bagels for a special breakfast.

When our family moved to Cleveland, I began attending the Orthodox Talmud Torah after school. They also ran children's services every Saturday morning and I enjoyed attending them. At times I was chosen to lead the services—a *girl* leading orthodox Jewish services! My parents were very proud, and their friends were impressed.

When I graduated from the Orthodox Talmud Torah Sunday School at age thirteen, Euclid Avenue Temple was one of two major Reform temples in Cleveland offering graduates a scholarship to attend their confirmation classes. I got confirmed there when I was fifteen. Going to Euclid Avenue Temple really opened my eyes. It was much more progressive than the Orthodox education I had been receiving.

My first successful "protest" was probably advocating for scholarship students to receive the monthly bulletins about Temple activities that the member families received.

After confirmation I went to Talmud Torah Hebrew High School. I really enjoyed exploring the old Jewish thinkers— both good and bad—although they were all male. In one of my classes, we studied Talmud (a record of oral law and rabbinic discussions) in Hebrew and English. I found many liberal views in the Talmud and in the collection, *Sayings of Our Fathers*, such as supporting workers with fair wages. Much of my activism for workers' rights and racial justice were supported by ideas from my Jewish education.

I started teaching while still in high school. Eventually,

I taught Hebrew, prayers, and Jewish culture at all kinds of synagogues and temples: Orthodox, Conservative, Reform, Reconstructionist and Secular. Orthodox are most observant of the Jewish laws, followed by Conservative, and the most lenient are Reform. Reconstructionist Jews connect modern meaning to traditional practices. Secular Jews focus mainly on Jewish culture. My parents were proud of me for teaching Hebrew.

My first year, I was in my teens and had no training. I was known in the Jewish community, so they hired me, but I didn't know what I was doing! I taught a kindergarten class at the Talmud Torah. I read stories to them, we did arts and crafts projects. I tried out a theory on them based on some reading I'd been doing about education. I told the kids that if they didn't behave, they could not stay after school. They all behaved in order to stay after school. Then I didn't know what to do with them while their parents waited for them impatiently. But the kids hadn't yet learned that staying after school was a punishment, not a reward. I eventually became a really good teacher and came to enjoy finding ways to educate children in important ways—no matter the assigned lessons.

•

I didn't experience a lot of overt anti-Semitism growing up, but certain events gave me the feeling we were not entirely safe. My high school had very few Jewish teachers; in fact, my science teacher might have been the *only* one.

One time he offered extra credit. The Cleveland Electric Illuminating Company would send out a light meter on loan to any resident who called and asked for it. The light meter would tell you how much light you needed to do a particular activity and then measure the actual light levels. Since I was doing poorly in science class, I decided to call the company and get the meter. I measured the light in the auditorium, which was used as a study hall. Our English class was studying *Ivanhoe* and I didn't think we were getting enough light to study this book since it was such small print. I handed in my report to the Science teacher and got my extra credit.

I was in music class when I got called to the principal's office. I had no idea why and I was scared. When I got down there, the science teacher was sitting outside the office and the principal called us both in. Somehow, my report had gotten around to the principal's office. The principal said I should never criticize anything about the school and if I did it again the teacher was going to be fired! It was uncomfortable and upsetting. It was hard to imagine the principal threatening a teacher's job like that—especially in front of a student—if he were not Jewish. I also learned a big lesson about the repercussions of challenging the status quo. You can speak up, but you'll face the consequences.

•

From a global perspective, the news about Nazi Germany scared me. When my family first moved to Cleveland in 1937, I sometimes heard a thundering noise coming near our apartment at night. I was truly afraid it was the sound of Nazi tanks coming down the road. It wasn't until later that I learned it was a trolley car.

In junior high, I collected scrap metal in the neighborhood with several other students. People put out old small appliances, pots, pans—anything metal. We walked all over, picking them up. Then we turned them in so they could be converted into armaments for the war. One time it started raining hard and everyone quit except for me and one other person. I was passionate about doing what I could to fight the Nazis, regardless of the weather.

I still remember very clearly when the U.S. bombed Hiroshima and Nagasaki. It was the summer after I graduated from high school and our "club" had rented a cottage at Geneva-on-the-Lake. It was a great beach on the coast of Lake Erie. We weren't part of the high school sororities because we either didn't wear the right clothes or didn't have boyfriends or didn't do something else right. Maybe it was just because we were working class. We formed a club of our own.

We were at the cottage on August 6, 1945, when the U.S. dropped an atom bomb on Hiroshima. That summer, my parents came to visit us to celebrate the end of the war. It was an enormous relief to have the war over. In later years, I participated in an annual Hiroshima-Nagasaki Remembrance Day to honor those who suffered from the atomic bombings and affirm a commitment to eliminating nuclear weapons.

While in high school, I joined the Zionist youth group, Young Judea, which was part of the General Zionist movement—not far right but maybe center right. I felt very comfortable and needed there; a stark contrast to my high school life where I felt like an outsider since I wasn't popular, rich, or beautiful and thin.

When I was about eighteen years old, the General Zionist organization provided me with a scholarship to attend a Zionist youth camp, Camp Brandeis. It was the longest I had ever been away from home, and I was looking forward to what I would learn. I went to the Zionist camp as a General Zionist but the young counselors at the camp had other ideas which were much more progressive. For example, they supported kibbutzim, the communal farms in Israel that I described in my paper for Mr. Thomas. I learned a lot from them and came back as a Labor Zionist. That is one who believes that a Jewish state can only be created through the efforts of the Jewish working class. The people who sponsored my scholarship, being in the political center, were quite unhappy about my leftist political development, though looking back I always get a kick out of it.

After the Zionist youth camp, I joined the Young Zionist Action Committee (YZAC). This group was made up of representatives from a variety of Zionist youth groups in Cleveland. One of our campaigns used fundraising cards to raise money for planting trees in Palestine. Each card had a picture of a tree on it with no leaves. For every 10 cents that was donated, we would paste a leaf to the tree until we had $1.50, the cost of an actual tree. The cards and money then went to the Jewish National Fund. It was a small gesture in the big scheme of things, but we did what we could to help the movement. Decades later I learned that many were planted over the graves of Palestinians.[1]

I later became President of Cleveland YZAC. I still didn't know where I belonged politically, but I believed in a Jewish homeland in Israel and was committed to supporting it. Since I had loyalty to none of the specific member groups, I was a good choice for president. It was a formative leadership experience and one of my first, besides teaching.

In 1946, I helped YZAC organize a picket line outside the British Consulate in Cleveland. After the war, rickety old ships full of Jewish refugees arrived at the shores of Palestine. Britain had a mandate over Palestine and the British authorities refused to let the refugees into the country. One of the largest ships was the *Exodus*, which the British took over by force, resulting in several injured refugees and a few deaths.

I was up late with representatives from different Zionist youth groups planning the demonstration. We needed money for leaflets, and I volunteered to call someone I knew from the adult Zionist community to ask for money. By the time I got home and called it was after eleven o'clock at night. As

---

1 *Washington Report on Middle East Affairs.* (2020).
"Jewish National Fund: Ethnic Cleansing Disguised as Environmentalism." March/April 2020, pp. 20-23.

soon as he picked up, I said, "We're having this demonstration in a few days and need money right away for leaflets!"

He said, "Why don't you young people plan your emer-
gencies?"

I loved the ironic humor of his response. Whenever I hear
about young people planning demonstrations and needing
help, I think of that. We got the money, printed the leaflets,
and held the demonstration. Our group was covered in the
local newspaper, successfully publicizing the issue of Jewish
refugees being turned away from Palestine.

The British Consulate also invited a few of us up to talk
with them. When we met with the representatives, one of
them read us a poem: "Poor Old Britain" by A. P. Herbert:

> "Nobody's wrong but England—
> and England's always wrong,
> Too late—or else too early—too soft—
> or else too strong."

The poem continued in the same vein, reinforcing the
Consulate's disappointing response to our protest; nothing
could have been done differently. Thankfully, some boats of
refugees were successfully smuggled into Palestine. It gave me
hope to see photos of Jewish activists secretly helping refugees off the boats and read about how they were absorbed
into existing Jewish communities.

I was also on the planning committee for a Palestine Youth
Conference in 1947. The year before the State of Israel was
established, violence and terrorism in Palestine were in the
news almost daily. The goal of the conference was to provide
information we thought would help people better understand
the situation. YZAC and the Jewish Youth Council cooperated on planning the event. We held the conference at the
Euclid Avenue Temple. Considering the progressive ideas
I picked up during my confirmation classes there, it was a
perfect place to host the conference.

The planning committee came up with challenging questions to attract people to the conference: "What is behind the 'scare tactics' in Palestine? What does Britain hope to gain by her recent policy in Palestine? What are the methods and motives of the Jewish Resistance movement?" We had interesting workshop topics: "Palestine Resistance Forces" and "Arabs Live There Too." It's hard to believe that we were already raising the Arab Palestinian perspective before Israel became a state—but I have always felt it valuable to be on the cutting edge. Someone needs to lead the way.

A number of prominent Jewish leaders agreed to be part of the discussion groups. One speaker, Aryeh Shindelman, was a leader of the Palestine Labor Movement and came to the U.S. as a special emissary to the American Zionist Youth Movements. We planned music, folk dancing, and other Palestine-themed entertainment. Back then, "Palestine-themed" actually meant Jewish. A lot can change in just a few decades.

Over two hundred people participated with curiosity and an interest in learning more. All of the informational pamphlets were picked up and read. The hour-long workshops seemed too short for the participants, who were very engaged in the discussions. People stayed after the conference was over to continue discussing—or arguing—and a spontaneous hora broke out during the arguments. We invited people to fill out cards to volunteer or to receive more information about Zionist organizations and got about fifteen back.

The conference really set an example for Zionist groups around the country. We heard about similar conferences happening in New Haven, Connecticut and Schenectady, New York. It was exciting to see this national wave of awareness-raising about issues in Palestine.

As I further developed my plans to live in Israel, my best friend, Karen Stern, and I went to a training farm in Hightstown, New Jersey called a hachshara. In Hebrew, hachshara literally means "preparation," and it was to prepare Americans who were planning to move to a kibbutz in Israel. My friend Karen was also a member of our high school club. She and her family were refugees from Nazi Germany. She was a good friend through college, and ultimately ended up moving to Israel.

This particular hachshara was run by the Socialist Zionist group, HaShomer Hatzair (The Young Guard). We worked hard in the fields and had exciting political discussions at every turn. Most members weren't religious at all. For the first time in my life, I ate non-kosher food. God didn't smite me, but I was seriously worried for a while that He would.

A large photo of a Zionist leader hung on the wall of the common area, but overnight someone replaced it with a picture of Karl Marx. Every night the pictures were intermittently replaced. This back-and-forth epitomized our political differences.

I also met one of my early romantic interests at the Hightstown hachshara, Natan Silverman. After the training ended, Natan came to visit me in Cleveland a few times. We fell in love and planned to go live in Israel together. Natan did move to Israel, but my dreams changed. Eventually, he wanted to come back to live in the U.S. and it became impossible because he had given up his citizenship here.

Before I departed for the 1951 World Youth Festival, I went to New York to meet with his parents. I told them I was planning to visit him in Israel after the festival. Natan's parents hoped I could get him back, but I spoke with lawyers before I left, and it wasn't hopeful. We wanted to get married when he got back to the U.S., but he never made it back. In the meantime, I met my actual future husband, Morton Frank, in 1950.

Discovering WILPF
and Family Life

Karen Stern met Mort at the same hachshara in Hightstown, where I had met Natan! Small world. At the time, I was attending a Young Progressives' camp up in the Catskill mountains of New York. Karen really wanted Mort and me to meet each other. They hitchhiked up from the hachshara to the Catskills so that we could meet. It went well enough that we kept in touch.

When I got back home to Cleveland, Mort called and visited me. He continued to visit me for a few years. I moved to New York, and he visited me there, too. I was living with my first cousin Rhoda in the Brooklyn area. We rented an apartment, not far from Mimi, who had moved to the area. Mort was living in Chicago doing his post-grad research for his doctorate. More than once, he hitchhiked from Chicago all the way to Portland, Maine to visit his mother. On the way, he would stop in Brooklyn to see me before continuing to Portland, and then he hitchhiked back.

Mort wrote he was going to come visit one Saturday on his way to Portland. He called me early in the morning that Saturday and I asked, "Where are you?"

To my surprise, he answered, "Downstairs." He had already arrived!

I invited him up to the apartment, which my cousin Rhoda

had generously vacated for the day. We sat and talked, and I made lunch for both of us. Mort was with me all day and I learned a lot about how he looked at life and his professional work. It was a special day. We saw each other all of six times in the next six years, fell in love, and decided to get married.

People sometimes wonder how I "balanced" my family life with my activism. It's actually difficult to separate my personal life from my activist life. Mort has been a lifelong partner in working for peace and justice, and my sons were part of the journey.

•

Before I moved back to Cleveland, my aunts and cousins on my mother's side had a wedding shower for me. It was a bittersweet affair. My mother came from a big family, with her twelve siblings giving me fifty cousins! The aunts and uncles were very generous—they rented a hall and had a kosher catered lunch in the New York City area. Everyone was pretty sure my mother wouldn't be well enough to come to the shower from Cleveland. They expected only my father, but my mom did come. Everyone was glad to see her, however, the first thing she said was, "Where's Charlie?"

My mother's youngest brother, Charlie, had died a couple years before the shower, and no one had told my mother. She had been ill off and on for a long time, and her family was afraid she was too fragile to hear about Charlie's death. I had advocated for a long time that my father should tell my mom about Charlie, but my dad was extremely soft-hearted and couldn't do it.

Then they had to tell her. The big surprise of my mother coming was overshadowed by her finding out that her youngest brother had passed away.

A bunch of my female friends, including Mimi and Rhoda, also gave me a wedding shower. It was at our favorite Chinese restaurant in Manhattan, Wo Kee. We drank wine and mai tais—what a good time we had, laughing and laughing! They gave me lovely gifts which I shlepped back to Brooklyn on the subway.

I left my job and apartment in Brooklyn and moved back to my parents' home in Cleveland some months before the wedding. Back in Cleveland, my mother and my aunt Esther came with me to find a wedding dress. To my surprise, we agreed on a very pretty cocktail-length light blue dress. White dresses were traditionally a sign of purity and virginity; anything else raised questions. But I wasn't interested in a traditional-style dress—white wasn't for me. If Mort's mother was concerned about me not wearing white, she didn't raise it with me. On a separate outing, my mother and I went to a dime store and bought a matching blue piece for my hair and a matching veil; creative and inexpensive. I bought ballet flats and had them dyed to match everything.

The wedding was December 22, 1956, at the Colonial Plaza in Cleveland Heights; the same site most Cleveland Jewish weddings took place at that time. It was supposed to be a small wedding with only the family being invited, but then my mother said she was really close with her local mahjong group, and she wanted to invite them. In a way she felt closer to them than to some of the family. She often said, "You pick your friends, but get stuck with your relatives."

Of course, my father said, "Well if you're having your mahjong group, I'm having my pinochle group."

I was sitting there, and I said, "Well, then I'm inviting *my* friends."

I couldn't invite all my friends because I had a quota from my parents who—as was traditional at the time—paid for the wedding. But I found a creative way to sneak in one extra friend. My parents and I talked about needing music for walking down the aisle and the reception. One of my good friends, Ruth Emmer, was not on my invite list but she played piano. She agreed to play piano for the wedding, so I was able to have her there. Mike was among the friends I invited. For years after, my parents couldn't get over how Mike, a Black Christian, danced the hora with the rest of us.

The wedding had a couple rough spots. Just before the ceremony, the officiating Rabbi sat us down to give us a lecture on being good Jews and keeping kosher. Even during the ceremony, he publicly urged us to keep kosher and follow Jewish law. My parents had evidently put him up to this. It really irritated Mort; I didn't care as much.

Later one of the guests got very drunk and friends drove him back to my parents' house. Mike told me about what happened because she was the driver. Someone was grabbing a pot for our friend because he was going to throw up and my mother yelled, "Make sure you get the fleishik pot!" Since we had a meat dinner, it wouldn't have been kosher otherwise.[1] Of course my mother would think of that!

After we were married, I moved to Chicago where Mort was preparing for his doctorate as a cardiovascular physiologist at the University of Illinois. We lived in a university-owned studio apartment. Before we moved, I visited my family physician in Cleveland to take care of birth control. He examined me and said he saw something disturbing and wanted a second opinion on it. The physician's casual attitude did little to soothe my nerves. He sent me down the hall to a gynecologist who barely examined me before saying, "Nothing to worry about, but you can't have children."

Can't have children? I was dismayed. Then he called back my doctor and I heard the gynecologist say, "Well that's true, yes, I see your point there . . ."

When I returned to my primary doctor, he told me I had

---

1 Kosher families keep separate dairy and meat (Fleishik in Yiddish) dishes, pots, food, etc.

fibroids, and it wasn't a big deal. They sometimes inhibited pregnancy but if they did, I could have them removed.

Well, I got pregnant almost immediately and then the fibroids went away by themselves, which is not uncommon. We have two sons, both of whom have children of their own. Mort and I became the proud grandparents of three smart, adorable kids—who grew into thoughtful young adults.

●

Mort finished his doctorate in Chicago and was offered a post-doctoral job at the Albert Einstein College of Medicine in 1963. I didn't like living in New York. You couldn't talk casually to people like in Cleveland. One of my early days living there, I was on my way to work, waiting at a street corner for the light to change with a lot of other people. I was used to doing this and I said, "It sure is a long light today isn't it?"

I got such a dirty look. That's what represented New York for me. But that is where Mort received his post-doctoral offer, so we went.

Aunt Sylvia (Weinberg), my mother's youngest sister, found us a basement apartment in a somewhat upper-class white neighborhood in the Bronx where Mort's job was located and where my Aunt Sylvia lived. A male Black friend came to visit us in our new home and Mort walked him back to the subway after dinner to assure the neighbors our Black friend wasn't "out of place." I was the one out of place there. All of the neighbors I'd encountered seemed too impressed with themselves and I longed for a more accepting, diverse neighborhood. There was no one around I knew or would even want to know.

We also didn't have a car and it was a long walk or bus ride for Mort to go to work. Finally, we decided to move. Finding affordable apartments in the Bronx was very competitive, so I got up early every morning to search the newspaper. I saw one ad for a basement apartment in a private house which was in a more convenient location. It had one bedroom, one bath, a living room, and a kitchen. I contacted the woman who owned the house, and she said a lot of people were looking to rent it. The location was great, within walking distance of stores and a bank. I was afraid she wouldn't want me because I was pregnant with Alan at the time, but she said, "You need it most because you're pregnant."

We got the apartment. My aunt was very upset that we gave up the apartment she had found for us, but this was a much better fit.

Alan was born soon after we moved to the new apartment. My obstetrician, Dr. Herbert Winston and pediatrician, Dr. Lewis Fraad, were progressive doctors at Jacobi Hospital in the Bronx. They didn't charge us for my care—we got "professional courtesy" because Mort was a Fellow at Albert Einstein College, of which Jacobi was an affiliate.

I had to have a C-section because baby Alan kept turning around, which meant he couldn't come out safely. The doctor was very reassuring and while I was in pain, I don't remember being worried. I recently learned that Mort and the doctor were worried, but they had agreed not to tell me during the procedure. When I belatedly learned about it, I was glad they hadn't told me. Alan was born healthy.

I enjoyed being a new mother and spent my time taking care of baby Alan and ensuring we had three meals a day. I walked with the stroller to the bank and a nearby mall. Sometimes I met a friend at the mall who also had a baby, and we compared notes on how our babies were doing. I tried not to gloat because Alan, my baby, could stand up before hers. Alan was always surpassing his peers, first with his development and then with his brilliant mind.

When Alan was fourteen months old, I became pregnant with my second son, Reuben. I was thrilled to be having another baby, but my pregnancy was overshadowed by a terrible accident.

While I was pregnant with Reuben, my mother fell down the basement steps in her house in Cleveland Heights. My father called me crying to let me know she was in the hospital. Mort, our two-year-old son Alan, my aunt Sylvia, and I all immediately flew to Cleveland, but my mother died before we arrived. It was in May of 1959, and she was only 57.

My mother and I had our differences. She was uncomfortable with my peace and justice activities. Although we argued about my friendship and alliance with "Negroes," she never seemed angry; just puzzled. By this time, we had learned not to let our differences get between us. When my dad was away working, I would visit her to keep in touch. And I trusted her. It was difficult losing her at such a young age, before she had a chance to meet Reuben.

In the funeral limo on the way to the cemetery, my father had the car stop at the synagogue where my parents belonged and opened the car door. In Jewish tradition, it was one way of showing respect to a deceased righteous person.

Mort had to leave Cleveland early for his job, but I stayed for the traditional Jewish seven days of mourning before flying home to New York with Alan. On the plane home, I sat on the aisle seat with Alan on my lap, next to a man I didn't know. The steward came around with our meals and said to the man sitting next to me, "You take the baby while your wife eats, and she'll take the baby while you eat." And this kind stranger did just that.

I had to miss one day of teaching at a Jewish secular Sunday school while I was away for my mother's funeral, and they docked my pay! I thought it was unethical and unsecular. For a while, secular Judaism was assumed to encompass pro-labor, pro-equality, anti-war, and anti-racist values. It was started mostly by Yiddish speaking union activists, Jewish working-class members, and Jewish progressives. My idea of what it means to be secular evidently was not the universal idea.

Mort finished his post-doctoral work in the Bronx and got a job as a research physiologist at Ohio State University in Columbus. We settled into our new home and prepared for the arrival of Reuben.

In those days, doctors believed that once you had a Caesarian procedure, you would need it for any future births. I was scheduled to be admitted to the hospital for a C-section on November 15—Mort's birthday—but Reuben ended up being born on November 16. It's funny how it all worked out: Mort was born on November 15th, Reuben on the 16th, Reuben's daughter Stephanie on the 17th, and our daughter-in-law Nina on the 18th.

After Reuben was born, we moved to a bigger place. Our new home had a front porch, which I loved. There were lots of families in the area and our kids were able to walk to the public school.

Since Mort and I had recently moved from the Bronx to Columbus, I was still looking for a local group that was doing peace and justice work. After getting settled, I was invited to a tea hosted by the American Association of University Women, not far from our home. *Would this be the one?* When I arrived, a Black woman in a stereotypical servant's uniform opened the door for me. I could see it wasn't going to be my organization. I was uncomfortable there with the fashionably dressed women and stayed a very short time.

The summer after Reuben was born, I saw an announcement in the *Columbus Dispatch*, for a children's program called "Around the World in Art and Song." It was sponsored by the Women's International League for Peace & Freedom (WILPF). It was the first time I'd heard of WILPF. I called the number from the newspaper article and got invited to a planning session for the program. I met Dorothy Blackman, an officer of the local WILPF branch, and her husband Charles, who became our very good friends.

The program was interracial, international, and for children. It was the early 1960s—a repressive time—in conservative Columbus, and the League was creating this program. I was very impressed, and I agreed to volunteer on the planning committee. It was the beginning of many decades of volunteering and serving as Executive Director with the U.S. section of WILPF. By my second year I had become chairman (yes, all of us were "chair*men*") of the program.

Reuben was born the previous November and was far too young for the program, but Alan was old enough to participate. They had babysitters for the younger children. The volunteers met in a church basement and held the program from 9 a.m. until 12 p.m. every day for one week. Each morning a different country was featured. The guests who represented their countries would teach the children a song, a dance, and a craft native to their country. The parents paid a small amount to cover supply expenses.

Unfortunately, the first programs did not include African, Asian, or Latin American countries. It included Western European countries and Israel. Even Spain was too exotic. But that would change over time.

I eventually became chief organizer of the program for a number of years. We started having an event on Friday night at the end of the week. The parents and public were invited to watch the kids show off what they had learned with singing, dancing, and crafts. It became a real challenge to the status quo because it gave credence to other cultures. One family actually walked out because of this message.

Even with its limited vision, this program challenged racial and national stereotypes. I prepared a booklet about the program and sent it to the National WILPF office; a copy also resides at the Swarthmore College Peace Collection.

Later, I organized a similar program that was more diverse at the public school our sons attended.

•

Once Alan started school, it was clear he was very smart academically. He was in first grade at a public school down the street from our house, and the teacher thought he probably should skip to the second grade. In order for Alan to be advanced, the school psychologist from the Board of Education downtown had to meet with him to see if he was ready. She felt it important to interview the entire family.

We had to be downtown at 9 a.m., and we got all dressed up because it was conservative Columbus, Ohio in the 1960s. Alan was six and Reuben was four. When we arrived, the psychologist said, "I'll talk to Reuben first."

Reuben, like many other boys his age, wanted to be a baseball player or a fire-engine driver when he grew up. But as they came out of the room from their discussion, the psychologist was shaking her head with incredulous approval and said, "Do you know what he wants to be when he grows up? A school psychologist!!"

Reuben's social brilliance has stayed with him all of his life, and it's a quality I'm immensely proud of. While Reuben didn't become a school psychologist, he has become a successful sportswriter and commentator, and a tremendous help to Mort and me.

Then the psychologist said she would talk with Alan. After their discussion, she came to Mort and me and warned: "He's certainly smart enough to skip a grade, but you have to be careful with these very smart kids; they tend to turn radical."

I nearly laughed out loud. I wasn't too worried about Alan's radicalism.

Reuben constantly surprised me. When he was about six

years old, I came home from the grocery store to find him fighting with his friend, Fred. I separated the boys and I asked Reuben why they'd been fighting.

Reuben exclaimed, "He called you a *lady*!"

Then he explained to me that a lady wears white gloves and high heels, and she quietly sits back to let others take charge. This wasn't what he thought of his activist mother. He was right about that! While I didn't condone the fighting, I was quietly glad that Reuben recognized his mother as someone who spoke out. Over the years, both Reuben and Alan came to understand our activist work and make their own choices about speaking out.

•

While Mort was working at Ohio State University, I decided to get my master's degree in education. I'd been teaching for many years but had never received formal instruction on educational theory or how to teach. I was eager to expand my knowledge as an educator.

One night at dinner, Mort, the kids and I went around the table with each family member saying what they would most want to do. I said I wanted to travel around the world and do comparative education; evaluating what methods and approaches worked and spreading them to other schools. Mort wasn't surprised but the kids were—they thought I liked to cook! I was surprised the kids were surprised.

I was able to take graduate courses at the university, but I had differences with one of the professors. This professor lived in a beautiful old house outside of Columbus and had a custom of inviting his students to his home for coffee or drinks. While we were there, the students would admire his house and he would enjoy their flattery. I was impressed with a swing hanging from a very high tree branch in the yard—I knew my boys would have loved to play on it. When I commented on it, the professor's facial expression indicated the swing wasn't what he wanted to be admired.

The first grading period arrived, and the professor distributed grades to all of the students except me. I went up to his desk and told him he'd forgotten to hand mine back. It turned out he had lost my grade and since he couldn't find it, he made one up on the spot. I was annoyed to say the least, but there wasn't much I could do about it. I think I rattled him with the challenging questions I asked in class. Unfortunately, we left Columbus for Mort's work before I was able to get my advanced degree.

Activism with Children

We found ourselves back in the Bronx, again! One thing I hadn't wanted to do was move back to New York. Mort had job interviews all around the country, but he finally accepted a position at New York Medical College in the Bronx. The opportunity was too good to pass up.

I went to New York by myself to find a place for us to live and left Mort to take care of the kids. Alan, who was about seven at the time, told Mort he was scared I was never coming back! I finally found and rented a three-bedroom apartment in the Bronx. It was city-supported, which made it affordable for a middle-class family.

Although I had successfully found an apartment, I had much more trouble with the schools. The kindergarten Reuben was supposed to attend was overcrowded; a fact the principal had not mentioned when I visited the school. I had to drive him back and forth to a school further away, although it was a good school, so I didn't mind too much.

Alan's new school required us to visit the principal's office so she could determine in what grade to place him. It was a terrible meeting. She handed Alan a book to read and he read from the book quickly and correctly. Alan was an excellent reader. Then the principal said, "Now stand up straight and read every word slowly and clearly!"

Alan tried doing it her way but soon reverted to the quick way he was used to reading. The principal labeled him as "retarded." She said he might need special education. Ignoring my protests, the principal placed Alan in a class far below his capabilities. He literally pulled out his hair in the evening when he had to do homework at a level that he had surpassed years before. The school was awful; run with very rigid, old-fashioned ideas. We had to get Alan out of that school to save his sanity and eventually moved out of the Bronx to do it.

Before we moved, I went to a PTA meeting at the school and volunteered to tutor third- grade kids. The PTA had originally planned for the students to be tutored at the school after the day had ended, using books from the students' class. I spoke to their mothers and said we should get the kids out of the environment where they were having problems. The mothers agreed, so I made arrangements for us to meet at a nearby community center. I also thought we should use new content, and produced my own teaching materials, which I shared with the other mothers. Several of them helped tutor, leading to an overall successful program.

One time, I organized a trip for the kids we were tutoring and several mothers to a folk concert in Manhattan. Every Saturday morning the *New York Times* radio station hosted a free live concert for children. I wanted the kids to experience that same sense of empowerment and solidarity as I did singing folk music.

When I asked the kids about it afterwards, they told me what they enjoyed most was going down on the subway because they'd never been out of the Bronx. I realized that the folk concert—which I had loved—was not telling a story that this group of mostly Puerto Rican descent could easily relate to. It was an eye-opening experience and helped me to incorporate more diverse materials when I taught and tutored.

•

Alan was being forced day after day to work far below his capabilities. After doing research, we visited Teaneck, New Jersey and decided to move there. It had a reputation for being an excellent school system. Teaneck's 1965 busing plan was widely reported as the first district in the nation with a white majority to implement a voluntary school integration program[1] so, we knew it had some very forward-looking parents and administrators. We learned that it was racially diverse with flexible and liberal policies.

The Longfellow Elementary School was right down the street from our house. Alan was put back a year because of his age and his social development, but things were working out well, more or less. Around fifth grade, they introduced what was called New Math. Each kid got a workbook, and they completed the chapters at their own speed. If they got everything correct, they went on to the next chapter and if they didn't answer enough correctly, they got help and repeated the chapter. Alan finished the whole year's chapters in one month. He zoomed through chapter after chapter. It was a struggle to know what to do next. Eventually the school system organized a taxi to pick him up every day from the elementary school and take him to the high school to do high school math. His ability to think and learn was really incredible. The Teaneck school district highlighted Alan in their brochure as an example of how flexible and effective their programs were. Of course, the brochure did not describe the efforts that Mort and I had to go through for that flexible solution to be found.

After getting acquainted with other PTA mothers at Longfellow School, we decided to organize an "Around the World in Art and Song" program there. The parents were interested in a much more diverse program than what I had done pre-

---

1 https://en.wikipedia.org/wiki/Teaneck_Public_Schools

viously. We planned to have countries that were truly from around the world, not just Europe!

This program was in the 1960s, still during the Cold War between the U.S. and the Soviet Union, so I found it exciting when some mothers wanted to include culture from the Soviet Union as well.

We planned for second and third graders to voluntarily stay after school once a week. During the first day of the program, a number of Black boys were disruptive and the principal, Mr. Lewis, said they couldn't come back to the program. He called their parents to come and pick them up. I was very upset at his taking this action. In the evening, I called the mothers of all the boys who acted up and said, "The principal had no right to kick them out. It's *our* program, a PTA program, and we want them back!"

The other PTA members who were working with me also supported them coming back. The boys' mothers were very appreciative of our concerns. They must have done a good job with their sons, as the boys returned the following week and things proceeded smoothly from then on.

For the final program, we wanted to incorporate Russian songs and crafts, but we didn't know any Russians in the area. Luckily, Mort, from his work as a research physiologist, was able to get help from a Soviet physiologist, Inessa Kozlovskaya. She connected us with a Russian teacher at the United Nations school in New York. Soviet children whose parents were affiliated with the U.N. attended the school. The Russian teacher agreed to visit Teaneck and participate in the program with her students. I wanted to talk to her about it myself, so we had a phone conversation. Her English wasn't very good; though it was better than my Russian which was nonexistent. She kept saying, "Leave it to me, leave it to me, I do it." I still wasn't confident. I wanted the local children to learn a Russian song I knew:

May there always be sunshine
May there always be blue skies
May there always be mama
May there always be me.

I suggested it to her, and she said, "I take care of it." I still wasn't sure if she understood or not. On the final day of the program, I waited in the principal's office with Mr. Lewis for the Russian children and teachers to arrive. Through the window, we saw two old blue school buses arriving. I told Mr. Lewis he needed to go out to officially greet the guests. He straightened his tie, put on his suit jacket and said to me, "I'll go greet them and say, 'Welcome tovarisch.'"

I said it was a fine greeting meaning, "Welcome comrade."

Mr. Lewis said he'd think of something else to say.

After the greetings, it was still half an hour before school was done for the day. Out of the buses came a flood of sixth grade Russian students, two music teachers, and an accordion player. With school still in session, we all waited in the classroom of an open-minded teacher. The local children and the Soviet children were wonderful together, looking at books, and asking questions of each other. The Soviet children knew enough English to have meaningful exchanges. The U.S. teacher and the Soviet teachers were chatting away about everything. It was wonderful to see.

When the auditorium was ready, we assembled in there. The Soviet teachers were prepared; they taught our kids the song I had hoped they would learn: "May There Always Be Sunshine." The guests held up large posters with the words in English and then in Russian translation. The accordion player performed with zest. Everyone sang. Next, the kids learned a dance about pine trees. Each Soviet student partnered with one of our students and taught them the dance.

I sat on the floor in the back of the auditorium with tears in my eyes—it was more than I had hoped for. When the program wrapped up and the guests were settled back on their buses, I went on to one of the buses and I thanked them. I told them I had been to the World Youth Festival, and it had strengthened my commitment to being a lifelong peace activist. I told them I knew only two Russian words: "Mir y druzhba," "Peace and friendship." The children clapped and I cried. It was a wonderful day.

I also did a lot of volunteer tutoring while our kids were at Longfellow Elementary School. One of my students was a third-grade boy named Gary. His teacher was awful to him. When she saw me coming to pick him up from class for tutoring, she would say, "Thank goodness! Gary, you can now leave the class."

Before working with him, I read notes that his teacher had prepared, which said he was a liar. When Gary and I sat down to talk, he told me his father was in the Air Force, and all sorts of stuff I knew wasn't true. I said to him, "You have such a wonderful imagination to think up something like that."

It was effective to phrase it this way: not lies, but imagination. Gary understood what was going on. I was tutoring him in reading, so I had him tell me a story about his family and I would write it down. Then I had him read it back to me.

Gary knew that *I knew* his stories weren't true, but he didn't care. He simply enjoyed coming up with the ideas. Gary was more intelligent than his teacher recognized, and I found him delightful to work with. One time he complained to me, "My hand is brown, and they call me Black." And I said, "I can understand that. My hand is pink, and they call me white." And he laughed.

One day I wasn't feeling well and didn't have a lesson plan for our session. The mail had come, including an article from the NAACP with a photograph of a high school graduating class. The photo showed an all-white class except for one Black graduate who was seated apart from his white classmates. I brought it in to discuss with Gary. He was fascinated and was able to read a good part of the article, which was geared towards adult readers.

Gary did really well. I met his mother, and she was very supportive. I invited him for lunch one day. His mother got him all dressed up, and he came to our house and said, "This is where you live?" I had a feeling that he thought I would live in a fancy house. He seemed to have a stereotype of the kind of home a white teacher would have.

Several years later, a few of us progressive white women were trying to ease race relations at the high school in Teaneck. There were bad vibes between Black kids and white kids. The kids were not physically violent, but they expressed hostility toward each other in a lot of ways. "Rap sessions" were popular at the time. People got together to express themselves and listen to each other. We decided to organize a rap session once a week after school for kids who wanted to come. We were hoping for Black and white kids, but for several weeks only white kids came. Then one day, a group of about twenty Black kids came, filling the classroom. They were talking loudly with each other, and we couldn't get their attention to start the session. One boy stood up and said, "Okay everyone, listen to Mrs. Frank!"

Then he turned to me and said, "Remember me, Mrs. Frank? I'm Gary."

•

While both my sons were still at Longfellow Elementary School, I became the chairperson of the WILPF Childhood Education Committee. As a long-time educator, I was very interested in Childhood Education. The Committee chairperson when I joined was a wonderful woman named Elise Boulding. I knew her from board meetings of WILPF. She was a strong Quaker feminist, author, and researcher who left a positive legacy after her death in 2010. The Quakers had a strong influence in WILPF, with many of our U.S. WILPF leaders being Quakers.

The Childhood Education Committee placed an emphasis on raising our own children right. A song going around in the movement went, "Let there be peace on earth and let it begin with me." The words made me mad: Let it begin with *me*? How about we let it begin with the war-makers! It wasn't my kind of focus.

When I became chairperson of the committee in 1965, I insisted you couldn't ignore the effects of society on children. You had to look at what was happening in the world, in schools, and the effects that peers had on the children. You couldn't expect things to improve by only raising your own children appropriately. During my time as chairperson from 1965 to 1969, the character of the committee changed. A more diverse group of WILPF members joined the committee, not just Quakers.

Despite our differences, we all agreed on opposing toys that promoted violence. Every year, all of the major toy companies brought their products to a toy show in New York. Retailers would attend the toy show and make decisions about which toys to carry in their stores. We decided to distribute anti-war-toy educational leaflets outside of the toy show.

A committee member from out of town came to stay with my family in Teaneck. Since most of the WILPF members I knew were older than I and more proper, I was worried about our guest's reaction to the hole in our kitchen ceiling. When she arrived smelling of liquor, I relaxed. Together, she and I went to New York to distribute anti-war-toy educational leaflets outside of the toy show. We met with mixed reactions and never saw any results of our efforts. That did not dissuade us from continuing our work.

Next, I helped organize a ceremony outside of Creative Playthings. This company manufactured and sold everything *but* war toys. Our committee gave them a Dove of Good Practices Award in an outdoor public ceremony. The award ceremony made it into the papers, raising awareness about the issue. Local WILPF branches in different parts of the country also organized ceremonies for the Dove of Good Practices Award.

Because of the work I was doing, I was invited to Minneapolis to talk about war toys and gender-specific toys on a TV show. To prepare, I spent time looking in the toy departments of major stores to see how toys differed for boys and girls. It was shocking to see such a clear distinction between the boys' and girls' toys. Even recently, perusing ads around Christmas time, I could clearly see how toys are marketed based on gender, trucks for boys, dolls for girls. Much more work is needed in this area.

Dove of Good Practices Award to Creative Playthings,
late 1960's, Manhattan.

Our committee also drew a connection between the cost of war and lack of funding for education. WILPF was very good about recognizing the intersectionality of issues. During the height of the Vietnam War, but before the war had gained major resistance, we had a booth at the National Education Association meeting in the Atlantic City Convention Center. Our booth included information about the amount of money being spent on the war every hour compared to what was being spent on education. We had so many people visit our booth that they inadvertently blocked another nearby booth, wanting to see our literature, buttons, and posters. It was amazing and gratifying.

At one point, two white, middle-aged men wearing suits and ties came up and said accusingly, "What are *you* doing here? How did you get in here?"

They were evidently meeting organizers. I said, "We paid $100 like everyone else."

They told us we'd never be allowed to come back, but we were able to hand out all of our literature by the end of the day, making our efforts worthwhile.

The biggest project I organized as chairperson of the Childhood Education Committee was to challenge the biased coverage *My Weekly Reader* presented to school children as news. *My Weekly Reader* had recently been bought by the Xerox Corporation, which represented itself as a liberal organization. It was periodically produced for several grades and had a Teacher's Edition with questions to ask the kids.

I developed questionnaires focused on how the publication covered issues of race, gender, and the Vietnam war. Then WILPF members around the country—mostly young mothers—volunteered to subscribe to the fifth-grade publication. They reviewed each issue, completed the questionnaires, and sent them back to me. I prepared a report based on their responses. The results indicated extremely biased coverage. There was never any mention of African Americans or Black Americans at all. At all! And they featured American soldiers giving little red wagons to Vietnamese children. This was to show how nice the U.S. soldiers were—as if they weren't killing the children's parents and families.

I wanted to talk to the Xerox Corporation about their publication, but it was not easy to get an appointment. I decided to contact Elise Boulding, the previous Childhood Committee chair, for help. Elise got in touch with Harold Taylor, who had been the President of Swarthmore College, and told him about the project. He was open to learning more about it, so I followed up and called Dr. Taylor. It turned out that he was interested in the meeting and agreed to be part of it. When I called Xerox back, I mentioned Dr. Taylor's name and I was finally able to get the appointment!

On the phone preparing for the meeting, Dr. Taylor was clear: "We're not going to argue with them. We're going to explain our concerns to them, but we're not going to raise our voices."

I met Dr. Taylor in the lobby of the Xerox building in New York. We went up to an impressive conference room. About ten Xerox staff were sitting around a beautiful, long table with a carafe of water for each of us on it. Despite decades of being an activist, my direct experience facing power was limited, and I still remained naïve enough to be impressed.

We presented our concerns to the group, and for some reason they could not understand what we were saying. "What's wrong with giving kids red wagons?" they asked. Harold Taylor finally ran out of patience—and *he* raised his voice. I loved it!

We did eventually get our point across and for a while we saw some improvement. The *Weekly Reader* carried a few articles about Black people. They covered a spectacular event in Mexico City in 1968 at the summer Olympics. Two Black athletes, Tommie Smith and John Carlos, stood on a stand to receive medals for their victories in the 200-meter race. Then they raised their arms with clenched fists in the "Black Power" salute. The *Weekly Reader* also finally published an article about the war in Vietnam that featured some opposition to the war.

Many people had invested time into this project and worked on it with me. I reported on the project at a WILPF National Board meeting and was met with excitement and applause. It made me a WILPF star for a short time.

A writer from the *Saturday Review of Literature*—a very highly regarded magazine at the time—contacted me asking for an interview about the *Weekly Reader* project. I was really excited and got all dressed up for our meeting in Manhattan. The writer took me out to breakfast and when I got home, I told Mort, "Do you know how much breakfast cost? $6? He spent $6 on me!"

That was a lot of money back then. For some workers, my breakfast cost half a day's wages (at the minimum wage of $1.60 per hour). The writer published a compelling article about the project in the magazine. I was delighted to see it also covered in the periodical *FARM & DAIRY* from Salem, Ohio in May 1968. We had other media coverage about our work but not as much as it deserved. It was an important project because it led to articles that gave children unbiased facts about the U.S. and the world and encouraged them to think critically.

My Weekly Reader rarely mentioned African Americans in their publication before we brought it up. This was just one symptom of racial inequality in schools.

I planned a workshop about racial inequality in schools with Marii Hasegawa, National WILPF Chairperson, to facilitate at a national WILPF annual meeting in Atlanta. I invited local activists who were involved in improving schools to join the workshop as well. I wanted passionate locals to be part of the event alongside WILPF activists.

At some point before the workshop, we got information about a local anti-racism demonstration from activists who knew we were in town. They urged us to support this anti-racism action in their city. Our workshop on racism was at the same time as the demonstration. We had to decide: "Do we have a discussion on racism or go protest against it?"

It was a classic discussion to have: "Do we talk, or do we walk?"

Neither Marii nor I could see ourselves saying no to the activists. We all went and supported the protest. Our committee had few opportunities to act together against racial inequality, so we found another time for the workshop.

One local activist who came and participated was a young Black teacher. He was very excited to be there, and I was very pleased to have him. He invited me and one other WILPF member out to supper at his favorite rib place. It was very special. We were the only white people there, and I felt it an honor.

•

As our sons were getting older, Mort and I wanted them to have the experience of a Socialist society, especially one that Mort and I appreciated. We weren't sure we could afford it, but our sons would be getting to an age where they wouldn't appreciate traveling with their parents. So, we went in May 1973, when they were thirteen and fifteen years old.

The heart of the trip was visiting the German Democratic Republic (GDR). Mort had met Peter Schwartze at an international physiological conference several years before. We spent a lot of time with Peter, his wife Hannelore, their son, Thomas, and daughter, Ulrike, in Leipzig. We had sent ahead a Monopoly game in German. Although Alan and Reuben knew no German, and Thomas and Ulrike knew little English, we heard them laughing together while playing. Reuben said Thomas was his new best friend.

When Reuben returned to school in the fall, his fifth-grade teacher, like almost all teachers, asked the kids what they did that summer. Reuben reported that he had been to Europe, including East Germany (I imagine he was the only one in his class). The teacher commiserated, "Oh, those poor people."

When Reuben described the Schwartz's comfortable home with its telescope, harpsichord, books, and games, the teacher accused him of lying! She described the streets as teeming with tanks and suggested that Reuben may not have noticed them. This is how the GDR was portrayed in the U.S.

Just as I had experienced being in the GDR years ago at the World Youth Festival, our sons had the opportunity to see for themselves what it was like, and how different it was from the media portrayals. It was a great educational experience for them.

●

In addition to tutoring and volunteering with WILPF, I continued to work in Jewish education. Teaching gave me opportunities to encourage students to embrace diversity, question everything, and push for social change where it was needed.

Mishkan Shalom is a Reconstructionist synagogue not far from our home. My fifth grade assigned class curriculum was focused on Biblical Prophets and Jewish holidays. One year, I got permission from the principal to take my class to an anti-sweatshop action with petitions and leaflets. It was part of a nationwide action against sweatshop conditions at the company that Gap contracted to produce its goods. One of the Gap stores was just a few blocks from Mishkan Shalom. I told the kids they couldn't go without signed permission slips from their parents. One boy came anyhow and assured me he could participate since his father worked for a union. I was delighted.

My approach to teaching the Holocaust at Temple Shalom was not met with the same approval. During a teachers' meeting, the Rabbi walked in as I was saying that it wasn't *only* Jews who were killed in the Holocaust. He said, "No, no, no, no. The Jews were the only ones killed because of their religion and that's what we must focus on; the six million Jews who were killed."

It bothered me that he wanted to keep information from the kids about five million others who were murdered: the Roma ("Gypsies"), trade unionists, gay people, Communists, Catholics, people with disabilities, priests, and prominent non-Aryans.

Despite his disapproval, when I taught students about the Holocaust, I told them it wasn't only Jews who were victims. Students were shocked. While walking with the class down to an assembly, I heard one boy tell another, "They don't want us to know about that, so we don't marry a non-Jew."

Somehow, he intuited the push to keep Jewish people separate.

I *really* got into trouble after reporting to a parents' meeting about our trip to the GDR. I shared some of the positive things going on there, including impressive actions regarding Jewish people. This wasn't what the parents knew or how American media portrayed the GDR. I was called back the same evening. By this time, we had moved from Teaneck to White Plains. It was a long trip from where we lived and not easy driving at night. When I got back, the Temple President accosted me about the presentation. It felt like a witch hunt. I was severely criticized for having positive things to say about East Germans.

I soon left the job because of the driving distance, but despite the warning, I left in good standing. Temple Shalom gave me a very pretty necklace as a going away present. Despite my habit of pushing boundaries, I was recognized as a good teacher.

Before that job, I was Principal of the Fairlawn Jewish Children's School, a secular Sunday school. I wanted my kids to get a positive secular Jewish education and figured the best way to accomplish it would be if I were in charge.

One of my primary focuses was music, of course. In addition to Yiddish songs, and holiday songs, our music teacher taught some Beatles and Bob Dylan songs. At a graduation assembly, the kids sang the Dylan song, "The Times They are a-Changin'" It included the line: "If you can't lend a hand, then get out of the way." A father stood up, took his kids, and left the assembly and the school—evidently prompted by the song. He got out of the way and became a school legend!

One of our successful projects was the creation of a secular Haggadah based on the traditional religious one. The Haggadah (the telling) relates the handed-down story of the Israelites in ancient Egypt: the plagues, the crossing of the Red Sea, and living in the desert for 40 years. *Our* Haggadah said it was the people who freed themselves from bondage, rather than God. But we are in solidarity with those who believe otherwise, as long as they support the liberation of all people.

I brought the secular Haggadah with me to other places I taught, and it also became our family Haggadah. Both of our sons learned a lot at that school. When they graduated, I left the job and went on to the Reconstructionist school.

The summer before Alan went off to college at Oberlin, we moved from Teaneck, New Jersey to White Plains, New York. Mort's job with New York Medical College had originally been in Manhattan, which was a doable commute from Teaneck where we lived. Then the college moved to Westchester County, New York, and it became an awful commute, especially with the experiments that kept Mort late at the lab. We bought a chair which turned into a bed for his lab, so he could sleep there when he had to work late. It was very hard on him, and we knew we had to move.

It didn't matter much to Alan since he was going to college, but it was hard for Reuben. He was going into eleventh grade and leaving his friends behind wasn't easy. Before we moved, all four of us went to visit the area and talk to the White Plains High School principal. We walked around the main street and were delighted to come across a small peace demonstration, which included some people we knew. When we got to White Plains High School, our sons discovered the marvelous running track on the campus. It was much better than the Teaneck track. They were also excited to find a Jewish deli, which we frequented after we moved there.

While he was at Teaneck High School, Reuben insisted teachers were always comparing him to Alan and expecting him to be as academically brilliant as Alan was, even if they didn't know Alan. In White Plains, he was free of Alan's shadow, and he flourished. Reuben's academics improved, and he even made it onto the school paper. Because of that experience, Reuben worked on the school paper in college as well, which led to an interesting speaking opportunity for me.

War Resistance

My very first paid peace job was around 1970 at the Peace Center in Bergen County, New Jersey. After volunteering for a few months, I was excited to be offered a job as full-time Director. Imagine getting paid for what I had been doing most of my life as a volunteer! We worked out of a main street storefront in town that two generous men had rented. The Center provided draft counseling, organized cutting-edge political actions, and educated the public about peace issues. I started during the last few years of the Vietnam War, so ending the war was a primary focus.

Only three weeks into the job, a young reporter from *The Bergen Record* came to our peace center to write about our work. Jim Wilson began our conversation by saying, "So you're Mrs. Morton Frank."

And I said, "No, I'm Libby Frank."

He said, "Our rules say you have to be referred to as Mrs. Morton Frank in any article in the paper."

And I said, "Then you can't have my story."

He was annoyed but finally agreed—and as I remember, the paper changed their policy shortly after. He began the article by describing my office:

"On her beat-up metal desk, circa 1950, are an open thermos bottle, some papers with notes scribbled on them, and a file box for 3-by 5-inch index cards . . . The sounds of voices—almost all early teen-age—drown out the street noise. Peace stickers, buttons, and jewelry are on sale at the front of the room."

Libby at her desk in the Bergen County
Peace Center, NJ, circa 1970

"'Pull up a chair,' she invites, 'not that one, it's broken.'"

The article described the work we were doing: a fundraising book sale, a "meager meal" in honor of a local resident who had furthered peace and understanding, (rather than hosting a full banquet—which seemed vulgar while the war was still going on—people gathered for a meager meal of cheese and apples; with wine of course), and a peace booth at the upcoming teachers' convention in Atlantic City.

Getting a booth at the 1970 New Jersey Education Association meeting was a big project. Considering the success National WILPF had with our Childhood Education Committee booth, I thought it would be a great idea for the Peace Center. We raised funds for the booth, one hotel room—for all four of us attending—and a truck to transport everything. One young man our draft counselors had helped was licensed to drive a truck, so he volunteered to transport all the literature, buttons, etc.

We deliberated over what to take—literature, buttons, posters? How much of each? What would be useful and attractive to attending teachers? The night before I left for Atlantic City I couldn't sleep, worrying about what I might have forgotten. Then I remembered—we didn't have a waste basket! I added one the next day.

We drove down from Teaneck early in the morning and met with a few volunteers from the South Jersey Peace Center. We worked until midnight setting up our booth—it was exhausting.

The next morning, four young women came in and opened up their booth across the aisle from us. They were staff members of a publishing company, and the books were already placed on the shelves. Everything had been prearranged and they didn't have to worry the way we did. We were jealous of how easy they had it! The women all wore navy suits and blouses with big bows. Very classy. Before the conference officially opened, the women with bows saw our "Teach Peace" buttons and came running over to buy our stuff. They were thrilled with our booth, and their support challenged my stereotypes about their sophisticated outfits and commercial booth.

After the event, I prepared a report on the project for a large gathering of Peace Center supporters. Inspired by the women from the publishing company, I went out and bought a beautiful, long, multi-colored skirt to wear for the presentation. I loved it and found that it boosted my confidence during the presentation!

Another early project was organizing a Peace Camp, inspired by a terrible experience Alan had with the Boy Scouts. When Alan was twelve, we were told by the Scout leader, David Levy, that he couldn't remain in the Boy Scouts because he wouldn't repeat the words "to God" in the Scout's oath to "Do my best to do my duty to God and my country . . ." Alan took the oath seriously and wasn't sure about accepting God, so he omitted the reference to God and recited the rest of the oath. Mort and I were very upset with the decision to oust Alan and jumped in to defend him. We demanded a meeting with the Scout leader and PTA reps from the public school who sponsored the troop. In addition, we obtained the cooperation of a Protestant minister, Dr. Henry A. McCanna. He was an executive with the National Council of Churches and a member of the National Council of the Boy Scouts of America. None of it swayed them.

The meeting was awful. The Scout leader explained why everyone had to follow rules. As an example, he explained: "If my wife and I were driving home from the movies late at night and I came to a red light, I would have to stop, even if there were no pedestrians anywhere nearby, because it's the rule."

I asked him, "What would you do if you had a green light and there *was* a pedestrian in the road."

He answered, "If there was a problem, it would be the responsibility of the pedestrian, because I would be following the rules."

I felt like screaming and crying at the same time. Our family supported courageous civil disobedience in opposition to the Vietnam War. In our household, standing up for justice was often more important than following rules. Plus, the analogy made no sense at all.

Despite our best efforts, the Boy Scouts refused to let Alan stay without speaking the oath as it was written. He was disappointed to end his participation with the Boy Scouts, but Mort and I were proud of his commitment to his beliefs.

After the meeting, I was angry and distraught—and inspired. I went into the Peace Center office the next morning and *by noon* had arranged for a weekend children's peace camp, open to everybody. I had possible dates, a place, and the beginning of an interracial volunteer staff. *I was determined to create something positive out of that negative experience.*

We had an excellent diverse staff and my husband served as Camp Director. The "campers" were mostly children of Peace Center activists and friends. Our Peace Camp didn't do everything the Boy Scouts did, but it offered a place to be outside, connect with other kids, and learn about peace work.

Another way we educated people was to organize speaking events. The biggest celebrity speaker we hosted was Jane Fonda. One day, someone from a national peace organization phoned the Peace Center and said, "Jane Fonda is making a tour speaking against the war in Vietnam. Do you want to host her at your peace center?" *Jane Fonda—at our Center?!* I wondered briefly if it was a prank call. Jane Fonda was a beautiful, famous actress who'd spoken publicly against the Vietnam War. The call was real though, and of course we agreed to host her.

My good friend, Lee Ross, and I developed an incredible plan for the day. Jane would be coming from New York to Teaneck to meet us at the Peace Center. We arranged to give her flowers on her arrival. Then we learned that Holly Near and Tom Hayden would be accompanying her. Holly Near was a wonderful feminist singer and Tom Hayden was a well-known activist and a founder of the Students for a Democratic Society. Lee and I deliberated and decided that just because Tom Hayden was a man didn't mean he shouldn't get flowers too. We bought a bigger bouquet and they each got part of it on their arrival.

Our three guests arrived in the back of a pick-up truck, so Lee and I joined them on the truck. We first stopped at *The Bergen Record,* the same newspaper that ran an article about "Mrs. Libby Frank." We had arranged for them to interview Jane, Holly, and Tom. On our way there, we were surprised with a police car escort, which accompanied us to the building. All of the reporters' desks were empty; no typewriters were clacking. The reporters had abandoned their work to come and see Jane Fonda up close.

After the interviews, we went to Lee's home for lunch and a rest. The guests were very appreciative because few hosts ever planned rest time for them. Lee and I both arranged for our kids to come for lunch so they could meet these inspiring activists. We sent notes to their teachers saying family was coming from out of town so they could take off from school that day. It worked.

After lunch, we drove to a college for an outdoor rally where Holly sang, and Jane spoke. In the evening, we had them speak at a church in the suburbs. The place was packed! A friend of mine was knocking on the window in the back. She shouted, "I've marched with you! I've picketed with you! You better let me in!!" But I couldn't; not a single space was left in the room with fire law prescribing crowd limits.

Jane Fonda was a great advocate for peace and justice. She had traveled to North Vietnam to see what was happening and shared what she learned. She also spoke about the connection between war, racism, sexism, and imperialism.

Unfortunately, most of the Peace Center supporters didn't have a global perspective or even feel part of the world peace movement. I missed the experience of collaborating with peace activists from around the world, as I did at the World Youth Festival. I hadn't been out of the country since 1951.

In the early 1970s, I learned about an international peace

conference for Non-Governmental Organizations (NGOs) at Versailles. The World Assembly for Peace and Independence of the Peoples of Indochina was scheduled for February 1972. I really wanted to go, and I was able to raise enough money to attend.

At the conference, people wore clothes that displayed the many different countries represented; it was colorful, inspiring, and exciting. I saw people from Vietnam, the Soviet Union—all over, including many religious leaders. One Russian man in colorful ethnic religious clothing was wearing a "Teach Peace" button I knew had come from our Peace Center. It was thrilling for me to see that our local work had spread internationally.

Many notable speakers from the U.S. attended the conference, including Jane Fonda, Coretta Scott King, and Howard Zinn. Representatives from the American Friends Service Committee (AFSC), Catholic Peace Fellowship, WILPF, and many other organizations also participated. I was reminded of these attendees when I came across a declassified memorandum from the CIA to the FBI describing the people involved in the conference.

Sid Peck, a major force in the U.S. peace movement, was one of the U.S. speakers. He told this international group of peace activists: "You can depend on the American people. We will never elect Nixon again."

I was politically active, and I didn't see any clear evidence that Nixon wouldn't be re-elected. Here Sid was talking to a global audience—including Vietnamese people during the Vietnam War—and it was misleading! When I got home, I wrote a letter to Sid asking him to retract his statement about not re-electing Nixon. I even got people to sign it. He never acknowledged the letter. And unfortunately, I was right; Nixon was re-elected that November.

Despite this blunder, Sid Peck made significant contributions to building the peace and justice movement. He started organizing resistance to the Vietnam War in 1965 and supported the movement's growth until the war finally ended.

A major part of the Peace Center's war resistance was draft counseling. One counselor was meeting with roughly 50 young men a week. At the time, the U.S. had a national draft, not like today with a volunteer army. The draft counselors knew the law and they worked with young men whose numbers had been called by the Selective Service. These men were not necessarily conscientious objectors; they didn't want to go fight in Vietnam for any number of reasons. The draft counselors told them what was legally allowed and how to get exempted from service. Every time a young man had success in getting exempted, he would bring in a bottle of wine. We kept the empty bottles on top of a file cabinet, like trophies celebrating each step towards peace.

One young woman, Randi, was still in high school when she became a draft counselor. She was the most assertive of all the counselors. She would go to the draft board, where the young men were taken to be registered. As these young recruits sat on the bus that would take them to their first military destination, Randi actually got on the bus to give them information. She would tell them that they didn't have to go; that they could seek counseling and object to participating in the war. I don't know how many times she was kicked off those buses, but it never stopped her.

We organized a variety of other activities against the war. One was our tea and rice dinner. Vice President Spiro Agnew was the main speaker at a Republican $1,000-a-plate fundraising dinner in a nearby suburb. The Peace Center, along with various other peace groups, held our own 25-cent a plate dinner after we demonstrated against the fundraiser, drawing a stark contrast between the wealthy people supporting the war in Vietnam and the needs of so many here at home.

Our sons planned to participate with us but at the last minute changed their minds. They stood at the door as we were leaving and warned us to drive carefully—it was raining. I got a kick out of them telling us, their parents, to take care. Sometime later they went without us to an anti-war demonstration in D.C. They were in their teens, and we encouraged them to participate in the demonstration without us.

•

Starting in 1966, many people across the country did tax resistance, including a good number of us in Philadelphia. New taxes had been added to the phone bill to help finance the Vietnam War. Along with other activists, Mort and I withheld a certain percent and enclosed a note with our phone payment every month to say we weren't paying the tax because we didn't support the war. We held the funds in a separate account for peace work.

We used a portion of the money we'd withheld to rent a bus from Teaneck to Trenton. New Jersey welfare rights activists had planned a demonstration in the state capitol and asked members of the Peace Center to join them. I was pleased that my teenage son Alan came to support the cause. He and I went to the Peace Center the day before to collect buttons for it. Unfortunately, very few Peace Center members joined us at the protest. They didn't really understand the connection between war resistance and welfare rights. Most of the people on our bus were women who received welfare with their children.

We marched to the state house and the Governor's Mansion. As we walked, we chanted, "Ho, Ho, Ho Chi Minh, welfare rights is gonna win." Ho Chi Minh was leader of North Vietnam, and the chant connected the two issues of peace and welfare rights. If the U.S. were not spending money for the war, there would be more money for taking care of people at home. Of course, it's a simplification, but more funds *would* be available.

We met a lot of demonstrators from other parts of the state; many parents who had brought their young children with them. We were all walking on the sidewalk, and if one of the kids ran into the street, a woman would run out and bring them back to the sidewalk. It didn't matter whose kid; every kid was every mother's child. I loved the unity of the demonstration; different types of groups coming together and recognizing the intersectionality of issues.

The Peace Center job was fulfilling. I worked with many passionate volunteers and took active steps to promote peace. We all celebrated when the U.S. finally withdrew from Vietnam in 1973.

The activists and I wanted to continue our work as a peace and justice organization. We saw the Vietnam War as one of many issues that needed our attention and creative actions. Unfortunately, support was lagging as many of the Peace Center donors didn't see the connections between war, racism, and oppression.

Desperately needing a vacation, our family decided to take a trip to Europe in celebration of the peace treaty. We left the Peace Center in the hands of the volunteers. When we came home from Europe, a few peace center activists planned to meet us at the airport to drive us home. However, our flight was diverted to an unexpected gate, and we never connected with them at the airport. We had no cell phones then to call each other.

We returned home to a long letter our Peace Center friends had written to us. It explained that the Peace Center had been closed by the board while we were away and everything had been moved out—the equipment, the files, the fliers—to the garage of the local Ethical Culture building. I was shocked.

I don't think the board would have dared to close the Peace Center if I had been there. At a minimum, I would have organized resistance to its closure. I kept the newspaper clipping reporting on the board meeting held while I was away where the decision was made to close the Center.

I wrote a stinging letter to the board. It was a very political and angry letter, confronting the board for being sneaky. Although my first response was shock and anger, my confidence took a real blow from the experience. It took me a while to get over the desolation I felt. When I did move forward, it was working with WILPF, an international, multi-issue organization with many members who recognized the intersectionality of peace and justice issues.

Part 3

WILPF and Middle East Work

The WILPF Middle East Committee is Born

During my time as Director of the Peace Center, people started whispering in my ear, "It's not good what Israel is doing."

Information had started coming out from Israel about its treatment of the Palestinians. Although the movement was small—and still is—Israeli peace activists arose with creativity and courage until word finally reached us here in the States. I was inspired by their bravery and was determined to learn more about the situation and to have open discussions about it.

So, I said, "Let's have a public meeting about it."

But some board members said, "No! We'll lose money; we'll lose volunteers. It'll be a fiasco."

After a while, it was clear that a number of people wanted to discuss it, so I arranged a public meeting. We rented a place, and I invited Dave Dellinger, a well-known pacifist, to speak. He is probably best known for being one of the Chicago Seven anti-war demonstrators and a lifelong activist for nonviolent social change. It was the first time anyone was discussing the Israel-Palestine situation publicly in our area. While many attendees appreciated the presentation and following discussion, some people jeered and catcalled. Others got up and walked out. It was a difficult topic, even for the peace community. Still, I considered the meeting a success; it was enough to break the ice for more discussions to follow.

I think it was the mid-60's when I wrote to WILPF saying I'd like to join the Middle East Committee.

Marii Hasegawa, the U.S. National President of WILPF wrote back and said, "Then you'll have to start one because we don't have a Middle East Committee."

That was the beginning of the current WILPF National Middle East Committee. I put the word out through the various WILPF newsletters for other WILPF members who were interested in Middle East issues. Dolores Taller, a WILPF activist based in Berkeley. was one of the first to respond and she became my dearest friend. She volunteered to write a welcome letter to everyone else that responded. A group of us formed the committee, which I chaired until 1980. Our first project was publishing a series of articles in the national WILPF newsletter, *Peace and Freedom*. Our first article was called, "Breaking Silence on the Middle East," because very few organizations were addressing the issue. We were resisting the "Shh!"

Other articles included, "What is the Palestinian Liberation Organization (PLO)?" and "What is Zionism?" We got a lot of responses to the articles; some were good, but many were critical. As controversial as this topic is today—it was even more so then. It wasn't easy for even the committee members to agree, but we forged ahead and began a much-needed conversation. Each article was written by a different member of the committee, with the rest of us pitching in to help.

We did exciting cutting-edge work that became a significant part of National U.S. WILPF. When a close associate of Yasser Arafat's was assassinated, we wrote a letter of sympathy—and we received a grateful response. Our simple letter got a lot of attention. Contact with the PLO was considered radical—and I guess it was.

In 1974 Yasser Arafat was planning to appear at the UN. The media ran all these stories saying he was going to be carrying a gun.

The Jewish community opposed his presence there and synagogues all around the region sent buses to New York to protest his speaking. Along with many others, they considered the PLO a terrorist organization because of its militant approach to gaining Palestinian rights.

I was the Educational Director at Temple Shalom, which was one of the synagogues that organized a bus to the UN. From my temple office, I covertly helped organize support for Arafat's presence. I reached out to a number of peace groups, urging a statement that discussions belonged at the UN—it was where people *should* be speaking. I was working on behalf of the WILPF Middle East Committee along with Breira, a Jewish activist peace group. Arafat did speak at the UN, and he didn't carry a gun.

Around this time, Allan Solomonow, a pioneer activist on the Middle East, invited me to a meeting at the War Resisters League office. I took a bus from our home in Teaneck to downtown Manhattan. I had never been at their office before but had great regard for the organization, so I got dressed up for the occasion. Ha! That was hardly necessary. The meeting was held on the top floor of an old and somewhat shabby headquarters.

Many activists on the forefront of Middle East issues attended; Don Peretz, a very knowledgeable author on the Middle East; David McReynolds, a stalwart pacifist peace and justice activist; a representative from Women's Strike for Peace; and maybe four others. Everyone else was much more knowledgeable than I was at the time. A woman from Women's Strike for Peace said, "I don't understand why you're trying to treat Israel differently than any other country."

I thought to myself, "*What is she saying? Doesn't she know that Israel is special?!*" On the way home I thought hard about what she said and then talked it over with Mort. That is when I began to realize that U.S. policy in Israel and the rest of the Middle East was no different than it was in South Africa, Latin America, or the rest of the world. It was an epiphany.

Allan invited me to another meeting that was held in a small private basement apartment in Manhattan. He wouldn't tell me much about it ahead of time, but of course I went. It was there that I met a Palestinian for the first time. I felt almost as curiously fearful as when I met a Catholic priest for my research paper in college. I'm embarrassed to admit that I really wondered if he carried a gun—although I didn't have the nerve to ask. This Palestinian was a representative of the PLO, which held that Zionists had unjustly expelled Palestinians from their land to establish a Jewish State. The PLO advocated for the return of Palestinian refugees to their homeland. He asked what we thought kept people from accepting Yasser Arafat, Chair of the PLO, as an honest leader. The discussion was compelling and added to my understanding of Middle East issues. Interestingly, Yassir Arafat did become an accepted negotiating partner with Israel and was awarded the Nobel Peace Prize in 1994 along with Israeli leaders Yitzhak Rabin and Shimon Peres.

As I was becoming known for my work with the Middle East Committee, I was invited to do an exploratory workshop on the topic at a WILPF regional meeting in New Jersey. I was incredibly nervous considering the emotional responses I had seen to Middle East discussions. It was a weekend-long meeting, and I decided I would just go for the day and then come home—just in case it went terribly. Other workshops were happening at the same time, but our Middle East workshop was mobbed!

I started by asking the participants what worried them about the Middle East and what they thought should be done about their worries. I had a blackboard, and I listed their responses on it. We found that focusing on *what should be done* unified the group! Such an approach was brand new, and people were very enthusiastic about it.

I can't take all the credit for the success of the workshop, though. When I first received the invitation, I called my friend Dolores from the Middle East Committee, and we worked out a plan for how I would do it.

At home the day after the workshop, I got a phone call from the chair of the regional meeting. She asked, "Libby, how would you like to go to the 19th WILPF International Congress in Birmingham, England and lead a workshop on the Middle East?"

I had never been to an International Congress before! After saying yes, I hung up and immediately told Mort the exciting news. Mort said, "Wait, I have a map!"

He got out the map, and I pored over it. It took me ten minutes to realize the map was of Birmingham, Alabama. What a joke!

The Middle East workshop at the International Congress in 1974 was more involved than the regional meeting. It was two days long; a few hours each day. I was told a past Middle East workshop had ended in anger, with some women so upset they actually threw purses at each other!

Members from the Israeli and Lebanese WILPF sections planned to participate in the workshop. A large Jewish group from Great Britain also planned to attend—I'm not even sure if they were WILPF members. The day before the workshops started, the Lebanese women and pro-Arab participants were concerned about my role in the event. They thought, "Here's a Jewish woman who is going to lead the workshop. How could this be a fair, unbiased workshop on the Middle East?"

Fortunately, I had support from several advocates at the Congress. Ruth Gage-Colby was our WILPF-US representative to the UN. The Lebanese women knew her and trusted her. She arranged for me to have a meal with them so they could meet me and allay their worries. At the end of the day, we were all there for a common goal: to promote peace. By the end of the meal, they seemed to understand I wasn't so bad.

Another WILPF friend, Lois Hamer, asked me to go out for a walk with her early one morning. She wanted to explain the history of these meetings and orient me in preparation for my presentation. Word got around. People said, "Did you see who Libby was walking with today? She's pro-Arab."

I also had help again from Dolores and a Quaker woman from England, who were both extremely helpful in leading the workshop. We used some basic rules to keep the workshops fair: no interruptions, taking turns—small acts of courtesy that help keep the peace. Two of the rules were somewhat controversial. The first called "Starting from Today," meant that the past was the past and bringing it up didn't serve our purposes. The second rule stated each member could only criticize their *own* government. We wanted to encourage progress on the issues and avoid verbal assaults on each other's home countries.

The weekend was hard, but we did it, and not a single purse was thrown! I was tired and tense when the workshop was finally over, and my silly humor took over. I said, "Okay, this weekend we did the Middle East. Tomorrow, we do Ireland!" Only the few Americans who knew me recognized that I was kidding. The rest were utterly confused.

As a result of the workshop, the 19th International Congress approved a fact-finding mission to the Middle East. We would report on our findings in conjunction with the annual Executive Committee meetings in October 1975.

Mission to the Middle East

In planning the mission it became evident that fact-finding would require considerably more resources than the League could summon in the short time before the scheduled meetings. It also became apparent that certain facts were already available—but what to do about them was the problem.

When Israeli peace activists visited the WILPF-US office, they raised concerns about the Israeli Section. Some believed the section was an Israeli government front. Others had never even heard of an Israeli WILPF section. In addition, the Israeli Section Chairperson was not sending the members' names *or dues* to International WILPF, which was required by all sections.

Considering the difficulty of these issues, and the short time allotted for solving them, we shifted the focus to women's priorities in the various countries: their status in society, their activities, and their aspirations. The Israeli Section happily agreed with the change, but the Lebanese Section objected. They considered that the mission would be useful only if it aligned with the aims of the League: "to study and make known the causes of war and to help abolish them and work for a constructive peace." As a compromise, we agreed that the Lebanon Section would arrange a program in Lebanon to best meet this aim.

The original delegation included Edith Ballantyne, WILPF Secretary General; Praba Rai of India, a WILPF International Vice President; and me, as WILPF International Middle East Chair. Unfortunately, Praba couldn't get the necessary papers from the Indian government, leaving just Edith and me for the delegation.

The Jane Addams Peace Association (JAPA) paid for most of the trip. JAPA, founded in 1948, was inspired by the pacifist work of Jane Addams. Considering that Jane Addams was a founding member of WILPF, JAPA worked closely with WILPF and provided financial support for many years.

Our plan was to fly to Egypt, then Lebanon and Syria, and end in Israel and Palestine. Our itinerary was going to be packed. We had WILPF sections in Lebanon and Israel. (Later, a Palestinian Section was formed.) We were also in touch with the General Federation of Syrian Women. Their objectives were similar to WILPF's, so we wanted to develop a relationship with them.

We already knew a few Lebanese members from the International Executive Committee, Anissa Najjar and Siba Fahoum. Shortly before the trip, I received a telegram from Anissa, Chair of the Lebanese Section, alerting us to fighting in Beirut and suggesting we postpone our trip. Edith and I agreed we really couldn't postpone the trip since we had made plans with many groups in the area. I sent a telegram back to Anissa and told her we were coming as originally planned, except for Praba Rai.

Edith and I agreed to meet at the airport in Beirut and if there were problems with either of us arriving, we'd meet at the hotel where we had reservations. I arrived in Beirut, expecting to find a group waiting for me. No one was there; not the Lebanese women or Edith. Evidently, my telegram that we were arriving as planned hadn't been received. After exchanging money at the airport, I found a cab for the hotel.

When I told my young cab driver where I wanted to go, he said, "I take you to a nicer hotel of my uncle."

I said, "No, I'm meeting a friend at this one."

He said, "You are like my grandma. I take you to a nicer hotel."

I insisted, and he finally took me to the hotel I wanted.

I was the only woman there and the only non-Arab. I tried reaching Anissa and Siba by phone, but they didn't answer. I finally reached a man whose name I knew from one of the Beirut churches. He got in touch with the Lebanese WILPF members, and they reached me back at the hotel to make plans for picking me up in the morning. Then Edith called.

Here I was, having dinner in the hotel dining room, and staff kept coming over to my table telling me I had a phone call. The other guests were staring at me: a white woman sitting alone, making and getting all these calls. It felt like everyone's attention was on me. I was relieved to know I'd be leaving in the morning with familiar people.

Edith was planning to stop in Cyprus on her way from Geneva to Lebanon to participate in a solidarity march. Turkey had invaded Cyprus, and Edith was asked to march in support of the women there. Unfortunately, her plane couldn't land in Cyprus because the power was out, and they needed lights for the landing. They flew to Beirut instead, but she wasn't allowed out because her ticket had a stop in Cyprus and her luggage was to be delivered there as well. She had to wait until they could get into Cyprus before she could meet up with me in Beirut. Finally, they got to Cyprus and the next day she was able to join us in Beirut. I was very glad to see her.

Edith was a real model for me. She always had some of us stay at her apartment in Geneva during international WILPF meetings and she'd often be up typing before all of us were even awake. Her husband, supportive of all our work, made us meals when we visited. He himself worked for the International Labor Organization (ILO), an agency of the United Nations.

One time we held an Executive Committee Meeting in a beautiful little town outside Geneva. Edith had arranged the meeting, the agenda, the housing, everything. It was a lot of work! After the meetings, a handful of us went to her office, including Praba Rai, my good friend Anne Nelson and her husband, Len. Despite the distraction from us meandering around, Edith was already working at her desk. A telegram had arrived inviting her to speak at a major peace demonstration in Japan—in only two weeks!

I said, "You can't go, you just got back from a hectic week!" And Edith said, "Why not?" and she wired them and said she would be there. Edith's passion and never-ending energy were an inspiration.

While we were in Beirut, I got to be friends with Siba, who was a Lebanese-Palestinian woman on the WILPF International Executive Committee. Her home was in southern Lebanon, and she wanted to take us there. Israeli planes flew overhead during the drive and Siba enjoyed teasing me about my apprehension of the planes. Then she reassured me, "They do that all the time."

Unfortunately, we were late getting back to Beirut for our welcome party with the WILPF Lebanese section. They were all waiting for us. They wouldn't start eating or drinking without us, not even the hot tea. Our delay worried them, and they were very relieved when we got back. Talk about solidarity! Here I was, an unknown Jewish woman from the U.S., and they were worried about *me*. It was very heartwarming, and the feeling stayed with me through the rest of our time in Lebanon.

When we were ready to move on to Syria, it wasn't easy to get transportation. Few drivers wanted to cross the no man's land that lay between the two countries—claimed by neither side. Luckily, Anissa had a cousin who agreed to take

Edith and me, but he would only take us to the Lebanese side of this area. We were supposed to meet the Syrian women there. When we arrived, Edith and I got out of the car with the luggage and walked to the nearby building where we had agreed to wait. It was a bank. When the Syrian women saw us, they came out of the bank where they had been waiting and welcomed us. We were very relieved to see them. Walking down the steps of the building, Edith and I confessed we each had plans about what to do if the women weren't there.

We became guests of the Syrian Women's Federation. They took care of our hotel, our meals, our transportation, everything. We had several meetings and also casual discussions with the women. They took us up to the hills and showed us beautiful green land, saying, "You see it's not just Israel who knows how to make the desert bloom." That had a huge effect on me, having heard so often the phrase that only Jews made the desert bloom.

The women also took us to a boarding school in Syria. If even one parent was killed in a war, especially in the war with Israel, the child could go to this facility. They called this the School for the Children of the Martyrs. Martyrs were considered to be any Syrian soldiers or civilians who were killed by the Israeli military. It invoked mixed feelings in us. On one hand, we knew the children's physical and emotional needs were being met—the facility provided excellent care and comprehensive education. On the other hand, we saw how this school was being used by the government to make a political point.

The head of the school was wonderful! When our U.S. delegation went back a few years later, we returned to the same school and the same woman was still the director. I gave her a copy of my booklet reporting on the 1975 mission— which included her picture—and she was thrilled.

Edith and I started on the last leg of our journey. Israel wouldn't allow anyone to enter with visas from Lebanon or Syria, so the visas were on separate loose pages instead. We were flying from Syria to Israel with a layover in Jordan. When we tried to find our connecting flight from Jordan, the person at the check-in desk looked at our tickets and said, "There's no such flight with El Al."

Another customer came up to the desk and he had a ticket for the same flight, so it wasn't just us! We had to book a different flight to Israel the next day. We phoned the Israeli WILPF members from the airport about the schedule change and they were very frustrated that our visit was cut short. So were we.

Since we were stuck in Jordan until the next day, we needed to find a hotel, but the airport would not allow me to enter Jordan without proof of my smallpox vaccine. Who would have thought? An El Al official walking by overheard our problems and came over. She told us about a flight arriving soon from Sweden. It seemed that a smallpox paper wasn't required if you were coming from Sweden. The worker casually suggested we join them and leave the airport as part of their group. That's what we did. Although somehow, I ended up at front of the group; so much for blending in! Edith teased, "She didn't say to lead the delegation. She said *join* it!"

We got out of the airport and stayed in a hotel. It was a nice break from the busy pace of our trip so far. Then we headed to Israel the next day.

•

Over many years, there had been tension between the Israeli and Lebanese sections. The Israeli WILPF members felt the League had not responded to their appeals to denounce violence against Israeli civilians. Some members felt they weren't given equal opportunities at International League meetings to present their point of view on matters concerning the Middle East. (The Lebanese members had the same complaint.)

Most of the WILPF members we met in Israel had come from the United States or Western Europe and lived in Jerusalem. We met with Malka Shulewitz, who was the chair of the WILPF section in Israel. We had a hint of Malka's perspective when she got upset about us staying at an Arab-run hotel. The meetings with Malka were cordial but did not have the warmth and camaraderie of our meetings in Lebanon and Syria.

Libby with Edith Ballantyne and Pnina Herzog, President of the Council of Women's Organizations in Israel, 1975

One afternoon, Pnina Herzog, President of the Council of

Women's Organizations, gave a lovely reception in our honor. We met women who were active in various professions and organizations—all upper class and all Jewish.

To their credit, the women were curious about our travels to Arab countries. They wanted to know how the women in Arab countries lived. It was foreign to them, having lived for years in relative isolation from Arab communities: "What do they eat? What do they wear? Where do the kids go to school? What do the kids wear?"

The women were also interested in WILPF and several expressed interest in joining. They were impressed with our visit to Lebanon and Syria and our intention of maintaining contacts there. It turned out Malka told them they had to apply to be a member of WILPF—and *that is against the rules*. She wanted to decide who was going to be a member! We had to be very cautious about how we handled the situation with the Israeli WILPF section. It wasn't until after our 1978 delegation to the Middle East that we resolved it.

We also met with the Jewish director of the East Jerusalem welfare office, Mr. Sebald. East Jerusalem was a predominantly Arab section of the city, having been captured from Jordan in 1967. The office dispensed financial relief and advised in cases of illness, childcare, and old age. Mr. Sebald spoke Arabic fluently and managed a staff of twelve who were all Arab. The entire staff showed a deep commitment to the work they did.

Lastly, we connected with people from the Quaker Service in Jerusalem. These volunteers helped Palestinians who were being removed from their homes to make way for Jewish settlements. They also focused on mending rifts between Jewish Israelis and Arabs in the city.

When we returned home, Edith and I provided a report for the Executive Committee meetings in October 1975. We described what we saw in each of the countries we visited and made recommendations about next steps that would support a just peace in the Middle East. As I was quoted saying in an interview with the *Jerusalem Post* (May 9, 1975): "In each place we visited, we tried to put ourselves in the shoes of the people we were with." It was painful.

We had no illusions about our delegation reconciling the conflict, but it was time for WILPF to think and act constructively toward that aim. Our trip made us realize even more strongly the impact of foreign economic giants—like the U.S.—which utilize conflicts in the region to safeguard their perceived interests.

We offered three main recommendations. The first focused on speaking out and acting in support of settling disputes, in recognition of the fact that military power could not lead to a just solution in the area. This recommendation included calling for an end to all arms sales to the Middle East. The second involved solidarity within WILPF globally to support forces for peace in all Middle East nations rather than taking sides. The last recommendation was to arrange meetings between Arab and Israeli women who wanted to talk to each other and learn from each other.

•

I did a lot of speaking when I got back, traveling within the U.S. and even to Canada. I prepared a slide show with photos I had taken on my trip and used them in my presentations. People weren't used to talking or hearing about Israel and Palestine. I was again defying the "shh" and it was nerve-wracking!

My first presentation was actually for a progressive discussion group in Westchester County, New York. When I finished speaking, one woman raised her hand and I thought, "Here goes."

She said, "That was the most balanced, interesting report I've ever heard about the Middle East." *Phew*!

With the cooperation of the principal of a Hebrew school where I was teaching, I showed a shortened version of the slides that was better suited to my young audience. I was even more nervous. This was a conservative synagogue, and I had no idea how my report would be received. Making Palestinians look human? Concern for all parties in the Middle East, not just the Jewish Israelis? At a synagogue in the 1970s? That was my plan.

Students from both classes were crowded into one room when I presented. For the end of the presentation, I flashed the last few slides on the screen quickly, one after the other. They showed children from each of the countries we visited, and I finished with a bold question: "Which children do you want to save?" It made an impact.

After I finished, the principal said, "We need more information like this!" I was both thrilled and relieved at his response.

Through all of these experiences, I learned again that in speaking out, one can find allies—and by not speaking up, you've lost already. But it isn't easy.

Delegation to the Middle East

The U.S. WILPF Middle East Committee decided to plan a delegation to the Middle East. We wanted to see for ourselves what was happening and spread the word on what real people were experiencing there. The WILPF National officers and staff were extremely supportive and provided financial support for the trip. Dolores Taller was my co-chair and Terry Galpin-Plattner was one of the trip organizers for this peace delegation in 1978.

We had a rigorous application process to select sixteen delegates. Years before, on my way to the international activist peace conference at Versailles, a WILPF woman on the plane commented, "Aren't these international meetings wonderful? Whenever I feel blue, I get on a plane and go to one of them."

We didn't want the people on *our* trip to use it as pick-me-up. Members of our delegation had to commit to reporting on the trip in any number of ways. On the application, we asked what they planned to do when they got back; where they would speak, and whether they could write about their experience for publications. We personally interviewed every applicant.

I should acknowledge that one woman we liked told us she supported WILPF's Middle East positions and identified herself as a lesbian in her application. We didn't accept her into the delegation. I rationalized that while her identity didn't matter to us, people we were meeting in the Middle East could possibly reject our whole delegation and our message. Based on attitudes at the time, I imagined she could even be in danger if she traveled to the Middle East. Another of our organizers expressed concern that she wanted to participate in order to spread her own message. Based on all of these reasons, we didn't include her.

Discussing it years later, we were self-critical. We realized that we could have found a way to include and protect her. Not to excuse the decision, but to put it into context, this was in 1978; almost 50 years ago. The culture was very different. Thankfully, we have seen improved understanding on the struggles against homophobia, along with racism, Islamophobia, anti-Semitism, you name it.

A few people involved in this book questioned whether this experience should be included. I think it is critical for people to understand that even the best activists face challenges that they may not meet appropriately. So, we keep questioning, learning, and hopefully evolving.

We selected a wonderful group of women from thirteen different states and ranging in age from twenty-five to fifty-five years old. Some participants were Jewish and almost all of them were members of WILPF. The entire delegation was white; we didn't know enough at the time to organize a racially diverse delegation.

I insisted that we meet a day ahead of time at JFK airport in order to prep for the trip. I arranged for knowledgeable activists to meet with us at the airport hotel. They planned to speak to us about the different countries we'd be visiting, the customs, and the goals of the specific organizations we'd meet. I especially wanted everyone to learn basic phrases in Hebrew and Arabic, just in case.

The day we all gathered, none of our speakers were able

to make it to the airport to meet us because of a huge snow-storm. We didn't have the technology back then to conduct the discussion virtually. Instead, we shared the knowledge we had with each other and entertained ourselves.

We also couldn't leave when we expected—all of the flights were cancelled out of New York. On the day we were supposed to be meeting Ms. Jehan Sadat, the wife of Egyptian President Anwar Sadat, we were stuck at the airport hotel instead. We sat in the overcrowded hotel dining room, waiting to be served dinner. We were there so long the manager came over and said we had to leave to make room for other guests.

We explained, "We didn't get our food yet!"

He didn't realize the kitchen was backed up to the point where we hadn't even eaten yet; he thought we were sitting and talking after dinner.

I kept in touch with our local travel agent, Caroline Parker, using the public pay phone in the hotel lobby. Caroline kept working, phoning the airlines, and she was finally able to get all sixteen of us onto a plane, making it only a one-day delay. We arrived at an almost empty JFK airport. We were practically the first ones there. The staff person who checked our luggage commented, "You must have a terrific travel agent." We did.

Our schedule was grueling. We were up working early in the morning until late at night almost every day. We read our WILPF Resolution on the Middle East to every group we met throughout the countries we visited. This resolution was con-firmed by the WILPF Board and had two main parts. The first related to the borders and recognition of two states: the state of Israel and the state of Palestine. This section advocated for Israel to revert to its pre-1967 borders with international guarantees of the borders on all states in the area. The second part encouraged negotiation between representatives of Arab states bordering on Israel and the Palestinians—with both the Soviet Union and the U.S. participating in the negotiations.

This section called for an end to all arm sales in the area. The last part was an allocation of aid for reconstruction and for economic and social development. If these recommendations sound familiar, they were the same ones Edith and I proposed after our mission to the Middle East in 1975.

We wanted to familiarize everyone we met with our goals and get their responses. Although the responses to the resolution varied, it was positively received throughout the Arab countries—with the exception of one group in Lebanon.

Our first stop was Egypt, and it really wasn't much more than a stop. The original plan was to spend three days there, but because of the snow delay we spent part of that time at the New York Holiday Inn instead. Some of our cancelled activities included a reception at the Cairo Women's Club, a luncheon at *Al Ahram* (the largest newspaper in Cairo), and a meeting with the wife of President Anwar Sadat. It was very disappointing.

We did have the chance to meet with three peace activists in Egypt. One of them was a Jewish Egyptian progressive lawyer, Shehata Haroun. Several years earlier, he'd come to the U.S., and I'd arranged for him to speak at WESPAC, a wonderful peace and justice center in our area. In fact, he stayed with us at our home in White Plains. We had cleaned up our son Alan's room and Alan had moved in with Reuben for the night. When Shehata saw the room, he commented, "This is the clean room?"

Oh, well. Housekeeping was not my priority then, or now.

It was a delight to reconnect with Shehata Haroun and he even remembered who I was—*hopefully not because of Alan's bedroom!*

Alternative newspaper writer Mohamed Sid-Ahmed came to our hotel to chat with us. He wrote a column for the newspaper *Al Ahram* and had published a book, *After the Guns Fall Silent.* Mohamed Sid-Ahmed was one of the first Arab public figures to talk about making peace with Israel. It was brave of him because at that time the idea was very unpopular. Unfortunately, Mohamed's editor wouldn't accept his articles because of the content. Thankfully, the law guaranteed him a salary in the job, regardless of whether his articles were published.

By the time of our visit, Mohamed didn't see it as much of a risk for Sadat to negotiate with Israel for peace and economic reforms. He said that if Sadat *hadn't* acted, it would have been risky. Sadat needed to make a dramatic move because his political life was already at stake. We spoke with many other people in Egypt about this topic and all of them agreed that most Egyptians supported President Sadat's move to negotiate with Israel. They explained that his action wasn't fully appreciated by the Western world and Israel. In Arab culture, the first step in resolving a conflict is to go to the other person's home and speak with them. In 1977, Sadat courageously took this first step when he went to visit the Prime Minister of Israel, Menachem Begin. This was a new way for us to think about it. Sure enough, by the following year Egypt had become the first Arab state to officially recognize and sign a peace treaty with Israel.

Many Arabs outside of Egypt—including the Syrians we met—felt betrayed. One man said to me, "How would you feel if Charles de Gaulle [the French president and military leader against the Nazis] decided to go and visit Hitler? That's how many of us Arabs view what Sadat did in Israel."

We stayed in the middle of Cairo and were astonished by the number of crumbling buildings in the city. Our bus drove us through a cemetery where people were living in the shelter of the tombs. It was called the City of the Dead. Poverty dominated the city and drove many of the citizens to support a move for peace. Many Egyptians equated peace with prosperity, because if less of their national funds were needed for defense, then they could be used to build up the country and support the poor. This mindset resonated with me and echoed the theme of many demonstrations I attended. We advocated supporting our citizens over spending millions on wars overseas.

The next part of our trip was the most challenging. The night before we planned to depart Egypt for Lebanon, we got a Telex from our travel agent in Cairo. He said that we couldn't go due to fighting in Lebanon—the situation was too dangerous. We spent hours discussing our next move. Several delegates—including my good friend, Louise—were afraid of going; and with good reason. We had to get more information.

Three of us went to the travel agent's office. First, he told us that only travelers on business trips were authorized to visit Lebanon during the fighting. That made me angry, and I told him, "We *are* on a business trip—our business is peace!"

I doubt if I convinced him, but then he told us that if we still wanted to go, we all had to sign a statement saying we were going to Lebanon of our own free will and relieving them of responsibility if anything happened to us.

I really wanted to call Beirut and talk to the Lebanese WILPF members to see if they thought it was safe to go. The travel agent said we couldn't call Beirut because Egypt's phone system made it difficult to call across the street, let alone Beirut. I wasn't convinced. I asked, "Where *can* we reach Beirut from?"

He replied, "The only place I know is the American Embassy."

I said, "We'll go there."

He said, "I don't think they'll let you call there."

I said, "You call them for us, and I'll talk to them."

So, he called and was able to reach them. I explained who I was and said we needed to reach our colleagues to see if it was safe to go to Lebanon. The American officer on duty said, "No, it's not possible to call Beirut."

An Egyptian operator, Emil, was on the line and heard my

story. He interrupted the American officer and said, "You're going to let her make a phone call?"

Back and forth they went with the officer saying he couldn't get a call through and the operator saying he could.

Finally, the embassy officer said, "Okay, but who's going to pay for the call?"

I said, "We'll pay for the call."

"Well," he said, "Don't bring anybody with you. This is a small office."

So, all three of us went as we had planned anyhow.

When we arrived at the Embassy, Emil was there to greet us. He made the call to our WILPF women. No one answered. We called the Middle East Council of Churches, no answer. I only had one number left to try. Before I left the States, an acquaintance in New York had given me her sister's number and told me her sister was a member of the Palestine Liberation Organization, (PLO) in Beirut.

She said, "Please give her my regards if you should see her."

I took a long look at the paper with her number and reflected on what to do. It was not official, but the PLO was generally considered a terrorist organization, and it was illegal to even speak with a PLO member in some areas. Here we were at the American embassy, using *their* phone to call a PLO member. After some hesitation, I gave in and made the call.

My acquaintance's sister answered. Naturally, she was initially suspicious, but she was very helpful once I explained who I was and the reason for my call. I said, "We don't know if it's safe to travel to Beirut right now."

Beirut was divided and conflict often emerged between the sections. She told us, "It depends which part of Beirut you go to. East Beirut is not safe. It's where the reactionaries and right-wing Christians are. But the west is friendly and safe right now."

I was relieved to get that information. We took a cab back

to Shehata's home, where the other delegates were enjoying a peaceful evening while we had been figuring things out. After we gave everyone an update, we all agreed we *should* go to Beirut. Miraculously, we got our plane reservations re-instated. The next day all sixteen of us schlepped our luggage onto a public bus to the Cairo airport and boarded our flight to Beirut.

When we arrived, the Lebanese women were waiting for us in a reception room with cold drinks! Our Lebanese members were very resourceful. They'd gone to the Ministry of Tourism —which was not busy, for obvious reasons—and explained that sixteen American women would be facing possible travel problems. The Ministry of Tourism gave us cars and drivers—*gave us!*—and hosted a dinner for us on the final night. We had a police escort for protection and to help us through the checkpoints every mile in Beirut. The guards were mostly Syrians and were called the Arab Deterrent Forces. We couldn't have gone nearly as far as we did without the driver in our car telling them who we were and that it was okay to let us through.

Downtown Beirut, the central part of the city, was the border between East Beirut and West Beirut, with no man's land in the middle. Lebanon was a market hub for the whole Middle East. When I was there, the stores were shacks with bare bulbs hanging down. The government of Lebanon kept promising to rebuild the central city, but it was impossible; they didn't have the money. No investor, country, or company wanted to put money into Lebanon. It was just before Israel invaded Lebanon; a time marked by sporadic Israeli bombing and palpable tension. Very early one morning a member of our delegation came into our room and fearfully said she'd heard bombing nearby. We learned later it was workers fixing a roof, but we were on edge the entire trip.

I was eager to find a way to inform my family we'd arrived safely in Beirut, but I had to be careful about what I wrote.

I wired Mort, "Beirut beautiful." It took him a few minutes to realize why I had sent such a message. He remembered the message vividly, even many decades later.

Before we met up with the WILPF section in Lebanon, we had an issue with airport security. The loudspeaker system announced that Libby Frank needed to report to a certain location of the airport. We all went together, feeling apprehensive and not knowing what to expect. There on the ground, isolated but surrounded by several uniformed men, was an unidentified package addressed to me. I identified myself and one of the guards asked me what was in the package. I didn't immediately know. Our group conferred and realized it was likely dozens of children-size knitted slippers. One of the delegates had requested them from TWA as a gift for the orphans we would be visiting.

I opened up the package and felt immediate relief when I saw the slippers. Evidently TWA had packed the slippers up for us but failed to label them. I later learned that if I hadn't been willing to open the package, I would've been dubbed suspicious and potentially investigated. Luckily, it all worked out.

The WILPF Lebanese section still had the same two leaders, Anissa Najjar and Siba Fahoum. Anissa and other women were instrumental in building a village welfare society in the Chouf mountains of Lebanon. Before this school was established, the girls in the village were not getting a proper education. The mayor of a nearby town had given the women land for a school—but many of the students were orphans and lived there, too.

Anissa took us up to the school, showed us around, and explained what the children were learning. We passed along the knit slippers for the children, and it was very much appreciated. Then we had a wonderful lunch that the women of the village had made for us. The children had learned the song, "We Shall Overcome," and they sang it for us in charmingly accented English along with a dance. These beautiful children were so full of hope! It brought many of us to tears.

In Lebanon, we visited clinics, hospitals, and schools run by the PLO. Most people in the U.S. didn't understand that the PLO did a lot more than oppose Israel's control over Palestine. In many ways, the PLO reminded me of the Black Panthers in the U.S. Yes, they were militant, but they also cared for their communities by providing free breakfasts, programming events, and supporting schools. The Black Panthers were known for fighting, but that wasn't what drove them—it was the same for the PLO.

The Lebanese WILPF women wanted us to meet as many leaders of the National Front as possible. We met leaders from the Palestinian movement, the Socialist Party of Lebanon, Communists, and Nasserites[1]. Many of the men receiving us did it as a favor to the women who requested the meetings. After realizing we were both knowledgeable and serious about helping, they gave us much more time than they'd originally planned.

We met with an official spokesman of the PLO in Beirut to learn more about the organization. He said to us, "We have adopted the position of establishing a state liberated by political or military means. We hope the Israelis will be willing to withdraw [from the land]. The PLO proposed a democratic, secular state but Israel said no, and so now a state is to be formed on land from which they do [sic] withdraw. Who has military power—Israel or the Arabs? Who has taken the land—Israel or the Arabs? Who needs guarantees—Israel or the Arabs?"

We specifically asked him about using violence to accomplish their means and he said, "If we are oppressed and our homes taken, what shall we do? I've been expelled. Give me

---

1   The Nasserites believed in the social policies of Egypt's national
    party

an alternative. If we never reacted to Israeli violence [with our own violence], you'd never hear from us. You didn't hear about the PLO organizing hospitals and schools in the camps—all free if necessary. Nothing like this existed until the PLO was organized."

Having seen the work of the PLO, I understood what he meant. In the U.S., we'd only heard about the PLO's violence, but while visiting Beirut I got to see the schools and all of the hard work they'd done to restore and support their communities.

We also had a unique opportunity to visit a PLO leader in his apartment. We noticed the apartment was sandbagged downstairs and guarded by armed men. We'd been warned not to take pictures during our visit. As we walked up the stairs to meet him, we heard soft classical music playing in the background. The juxtaposition of armed men and classical music was surprising. After the pleasantries, I read him our statement on the Middle East, and I said we believed in solving problems non-violently. He laughed, somewhat bitterly.

His father was a Gandhian and had saved a leader on the opposing side from assassination. That was the family he came from; yet he laughed when I talked about non-violence.

He said, "What do you want us to do? With the help of the Syrians, we have to solve the problem of the Palestinians. Yes, the whole Arab world must accept the State of Israel, but the State of Israel must support the national rights of the Palestinians. Israel and the U.S. must recognize the Palestinian Liberation Organization."

We agreed that Israel and the U.S. needed to recognize the PLO, but also pointed out that the PLO's violent tactics were part of the reason it couldn't happen. In 1987 the U.S. officially designated the PLO as a terrorist organization based on their international terrorist attacks and murder of American citizens. It would not be until 1993 that the PLO publicly recognized Israel's right to exist and pledged to stop terrorism.

We soon ended our meeting with the leader and began making our way back down the stairs. Despite being warned not to take pictures, one of our delegates, who was an avid photographer, lifted her camera to take a picture of the armed guards. Luckily, I was walking with her, and I knocked her arm down! The armed guards downstairs saw it happen and nodded their approval. I can only imagine what would have happened if she had succeeded in taking the picture.

After Lebanon, we departed for Syria. Today it is difficult to imagine how beautiful Syria was in 1978. It hadn't yet been ravaged by war and poverty. It still took us an extra two hours to get there from Beirut because the bus had to detour around shelling on the main road. Instead, we took a four-hour circuitous route around the mountains. To make matters worse, when we got to Damascus, I realized I didn't have my luggage. I thought it would be picked up at our door, as it often was, so I left it there! Our Lebanese bus driver made a special trip the next day and drove all the way around the mountains again to bring my suitcase from Beirut to Damascus. I was so grateful.

When we arrived at the border, the Syrian Women's Federation was there to greet us. First, they took us to the School for the Children of the Martyrs. This was the same school I'd visited in 1975 when I was last in Syria.

Then we visited a girls' vocational school in Damascus, which I had also seen on my last trip. It was progressive then for girls to take technical courses to prepare to be scientists or technicians. When I was last at the school, I had asked the girls through an interpreter, "Now that girls can take math and science and all of these other courses, what do you want to be when you graduate?"

Last time, they all said they wanted to be teachers. I was disappointed to hear they saw teaching as their only choice. As a teacher myself for many years, I had great respect for the occupation, but I had hoped the girls would imagine a variety of options. When I was in school, women could rarely imagine a career other than a teacher, secretary, or nurse. These were the *only* possibilities they saw for their future. This time I asked the same question and was pleased to hear very different responses. The girls said they wanted to be architects, doctors, teachers, and all kinds of diverse occupations. It was an exciting development!

Our hosts had arranged for us to meet with the head of the Syrian Socialist Baath party and some of their leaders. This was the only major political party in Syria at the time. We were sitting around a long table with several Baath men and some of the Syrian women who were hosting us. We were allotted a short amount of time to talk and then had a restaurant reservation for dinner afterwards. The men had assumed that we were dilettantes. They were very surprised to hear our intelligent questions and concerns.

We ended up talking with them for several hours. It was 10 p.m. and we still hadn't made it to dinner! This was the kind of schedule we kept every day. Our hosts kept calling the restaurant imploring the owner to keep it open for us. By the time we finished our meeting, the restaurant had closed, but they opened back up for us when we finally arrived there for dinner.

At the restaurant, the Syrian women sat across the table from our delegation. It was another situation where I was so tired that I became silly. I knew that it was a custom in Arab countries that if you admire an item belonging to someone, they will offer it to you. So, you have to be very careful how you phrase compliments. For example, you might say, "Your beautiful necklace must be very dear to you; someone special must have given it to you," or you'll find yourself walking away with a polite woman's jewelry. As I was eating dinner, I said to the Syrian woman across from me, "I like your husband."

It was very quiet on both sides of the table. The Syrian women eventually understood I was joking and started laughing. Only then did the U.S. women resume breathing and join in the laughter.

Often when we spoke with Arabs, they couldn't understand that being Jewish was more than a religion, or that the Jewish community considers itself as a people with a culture and a common heritage. They understood observing Jewish religious rules, but why a state? The Christians didn't have a state. We were able to have productive conversations on this topic with the Syrian women who hosted us.

Another frequent topic was whether the American media was controlled by Jews. All of the news they saw from the U.S. had a pro-Israel and pro-Zionist bias, so they assumed the news was controlled by Jewish people. One of the women in our group was a strong Zionist; she planned on moving to Israel to live there. When it was her turn to speak, she said, "I'm a Zionist and I want you to know not all Zionists agree with oppressing the Palestinians or agree with the settlement on the West Bank. Many of us agree with a Palestinian state and national determination for the Palestinians."

I think it still surprised our hosts that some of us could be Jewish and Zionist while supporting a Palestinian state.

We had asked to see the Jewish community in Damascus and our hosts arranged for us to visit the Jewish section. We met the elderly head of the Syrian Jewish community, along with several other men. We didn't learn much from this leader; he turned aside our serious questions with jokes, and we didn't want to embarrass him by insisting he answer. He kept referring to a group of young Jewish Orthodox Syrian women who had traveled to the United States and found husbands among the Jewish community in Brooklyn. He wanted to find more husbands for the women to marry. It's all we could get him to talk about.

We asked, "Where are the women? We'd like to meet with them, too.""

And he said, "They're busy."

We had more interesting discussions with the rabbi in the community, especially because our group was mixed: Zionists, non-Zionists, Jews, and non-Jews. We never got to meet or talk with the Jewish women there; they were always "too busy" to see us.

We did get to observe Jewish artisans at work hammering gold and silver pieces. They were all girls and young women. I was fascinated by their skill and the intricate beauty of their pieces. Our delegation secretly bought me a beautiful plate from them as a surprise gift. They had noticed how entranced I was watching the young women at their craft and wanted to thank me for my work organizing the trip.

Hammered metal plate made by young Jewish Syrian women and gifted to Libby by the delegation, 1978

Since Hafez al-Assad came to power as Syrian President, there'd been an improvement in the situation with the Jewish population. In the past, Jewish people were required to carry identification cards with "Jew" written on them, but the policy was gone. The Jewish people became free to travel within the country and to buy or rent homes outside of the Jewish quarter, which they couldn't do before. However, they still weren't free to leave Syria. The logic was that if Jews could leave the country, they'd go to Israel and fight Syria. We learned that in times of peace, the situation for the Syrian-Jewish population was tolerable. In times of war, that wasn't the case.

The Syrian government was also making improvements for poor people. They were tearing down terrible shacks where poor people lived and replacing them with new houses for no additional rent.

On the other hand, Syrians cooperated with the Phalangists—a fascist political party—to attack the Palestinians. When I first met with the Syrian Women's Federation in 1975, the Palestinian and Syrian women appeared to be equals. This time, the Palestinian women sat in the back and played no role. The politics seemed to have changed.

From Syria, we journeyed to Jordan. Months before the trip, I'd called the Muslim Association in New York to make sure there were no Muslim holidays happening at the time of our trip. I was told, "No, no. No holidays then. It's all clear."

When we got to Jordan, I called our contact who said, "Yes, we were expecting you to call. It's a Muslim holiday, but we're going to pick you up anyway."

It was Mohammed's birthday, a major holiday. *So much for planning ahead!*

Our hosts took off from their holiday to provide a bus for us and show us around. We saw several incredible ancient sites in Jordan.

We also visited centers for vocational training. Jordan

had a labor shortage; with trained people leaving Jordan for prospects in other countries. The government was desperately trying to encourage people to stay. We met the female principal of a vocational training center for girls run by UNRRA, the United Nations Relief and Rehabilitation Administration. She had taken a year off to start a women's department within the Ministry of Labor. They needed to integrate women into the labor force in order to decrease the labor shortage. Inexplicably, no one even considered allowing Palestinian refugees to get jobs. Instead, Jordan's industries struggled with the labor shortage and the refugees were forced to sit and wait for their situation to change.

We visited a Palestinian refugee camp, and it was awful. It was *packed* with tents—crowded and dirty. Flies were everywhere. We didn't talk to anyone. We just drove through. It was hard even observing the situation.

The refugees weren't allowed to engage in any political activities. They had no PLO or political organization of any kind to support them. An independent political system would have enabled them to develop self-reliance and grow their community. Instead, they became increasingly dependent on UNRRA.

When we were leaving Jordan to cross into Israel, all of the literature we'd gathered in the Arab states was taken. Our shoes were taken too, but they gave those back. Some of the information we wanted to share with the Israelis was taken and not given back. Since we were Americans we made it through the border, but we saw many Arabs trying to cross from Jordan to Israel: people in hot buses, people on foot, old people, young people, waiting and waiting to be let across the border.

Although we were in Israel a short time, one reality was expressed to us over and over again: a profound fear that the state of Israel would be destroyed. This fear has been deepened in recent years by the tensions in the region. However, it appears to some Israelis that those in power in Israel are using this fear to stay in power.

In Old Jerusalem, we met with Felicia Langer, a courageous Jewish lawyer, in her small office. She was committed to improving Israel for all its citizens, Arabs and Jews alike. She provided legal defense for those who opposed the occupation, whether they were Palestinians or Jewish Israelis. We weren't there long; we were keeping her from her work; but she was very gracious to spend time with us.

She told us, "I'm the real patriot. I love my country and want to live here, but the occupation is spoiling my people. There is a growth of chauvinism and whatever else is needed to help keep people under occupation."

She described the occupation and rising tensions as making Jews into prison guards and Arabs into bomb throwers. Ms. Langer expressed her worry that the world would no longer be able to distinguish between "good Jews" and "bad Jews." She told us people didn't listen to what she had to say about the Palestinians or about the Israeli government because she was a member of the Communist Party of Israel. They dismissed her because they believed she owed her allegiance to Moscow instead of Israel. It reminded me of the difficulties I had back home during the Red Scare.

As our delegation left her office, I stayed behind a minute and whispered to her in Hebrew, "Ani Chavera," which literally means, "I am a friend" or "I am a comrade." She also understood my veiled implication, "I am a Communist."

In those words, I conveyed my support for her work and my own affiliations. We shared a moment of camaraderie before I left her office. Felicia eventually moved to Paris because she couldn't tolerate the harassment any longer.

That afternoon, we went to the Knesset, the Israeli parliament. You couldn't get into the building without an appointment and a body search. They were very security conscious. We met with a mayor who was one of two Knesset members from the Peace Party in Israel. Their position was that this land—meaning the land encompassing the occupied territories and Israel—was the land of two peoples: the Palestinians *and* the Jewish people. It was a radical thought for a member of the Israeli parliament, and we admired his bravery.

When we read him WILPF's resolution, his candor surprised me. He said, "It's what we believe, too, but it's a dream. The Arab leaders—even the nationalistic ones—see there's no way to annihilate Israel. They might be willing to negotiate but the attitudes in Israel are getting worse."

At six o'clock, we met with a leading spokesperson of the Knesset. She was a member of the Labor Party, which was out of power but part of the Knesset because Israel has proportional representation. In Israel, the Orthodox religious community determined much of the laws governing family life—such as divorce laws, education, and abortion—which often put women at a disadvantage. They also placed restrictions on what people were allowed to do during Jewish holidays; for example, driving was not allowed during the Sabbath. When we asked if change was possible, she replied: "We cannot challenge religious laws while our country is at war. We cannot jeopardize national unity until our country is secure."

She explained that the Labor Party believed there could be a West Bank "state" affiliated with Jordan but not an independent Palestine. The Likud Party (Menachem Begin's right-wing party) would not go even that far. We heard both a member of the Peace Party and a member of the Labor Party say that no one but a few Communists felt there should be a separate Palestinian state. Remember that was 1978. Some things can change for the better, albeit slowly.

During our trip to the West Bank, we were instructed not to photograph anyone because the people we were going to see were banned from speaking politically to outsiders. It was considered a provocation; and we spoke with several people who'd been jailed for this reason.

We met a marvelous Palestinian woman who started an organization to teach women how to become economically independent. While the organization was empowering women, the reasoning for it was fear and not liberation. The law stated that if land were left unworked, the Israeli government could come and take it, so men had to stay behind to farm the land. The women were needed to financially support their families, sometimes with jobs in Israel.

We visited Nazareth—the largest Arab city in Israel—and met with a group called the Nazareth Women's Fellowship. Practically everyone in Nazareth spoke Hebrew as well as Arabic. We learned that they considered themselves Arab Israelis. They were loyal to Israel, but they were upset at the unequal value they got for their tax dollars. They paid the same taxes as Jewish towns, but their services were cut tremendously. As an example, their public transportation options were much more limited. They were also resentful about Israel appropriating land from Nazareth proper to build Upper Nazareth and other Jewish communities. It was interesting to hear their perspective as Israelis, compared to Arabs in the West Bank and surrounding countries.

We got to visit a left-wing kibbutz. We were told 98% of the people living on the kibbutz opposed the Israeli settlements on Palestinian land; *that was an astounding majority!* We asked what they were doing about it and how they made their beliefs known. They responded saying representatives in the Knesset would speak for them. It wasn't common practice in Israel for people to become political activists. Most actions were taken exclusively within the political parties.

We could not imagine relying on government representatives to move our peace agenda forward. We asked, "Aren't there any other ways you can demonstrate your opposition?"

They could not imagine doing more than that.

Remembering how the Israeli WILPF section was accused of being a government front, I wondered if this mindset was part of the problem.

We later learned that some kibbutzniks *had* participated in demonstrations. Since they were not violent demonstrations, they didn't attract the attention of Western media, so we never saw them back home.

We also met with the Israeli Black Panthers, a group inspired by the Black Panthers in the U.S., which was active during the Civil Rights Movement. In Israel, "Black Panther" was used as a derogatory term for the African Jews living in Israel. The group reclaimed the name and created a movement to protest discrimination against African and Mizrahi Jews.[2] We appreciated the Black Panthers' commitment to equality regardless of religion, race, or ethnicity.

Early one evening, we had a meeting with the Israeli section of an international organization called the World Federation of Democratic Women. It was a progressive group made up of Jewish and Arab women, unlike the existing all-Jewish WILPF Section. One leader was an Arab woman named Zamirah, who was from Nazareth. We discussed our group's goals and different actions we took for social change, and we had the opportunity to exchange ideas.

Zamirah excused herself from the meeting for a few minutes and when she came back, she pulled me aside to tell me that a few Jewish and Arab women of the group called Gesher L'Shalom (Bridge to Peace) were waiting downstairs. They had heard we'd be in Israel and had come from different parts of Israel to meet us. Zamirah urged us to end the

---

2 When the state of Israel was created, many Jews living in the surrounding Muslim or Arab countries were expelled or chose to leave their countries due to anti-Jewish government actions. Known as Mizrachi Jews, they became refugees, and many emigrated to Israel where, ironically, they were subject to discrimination.

meeting with the World Federation of Democratic Women, quickly but politely, so Gesher L'Shalom could come up to join us. It was difficult to do so tactfully, but I think we succeeded.

Almost immediately after they left, the women from Gesher L'Shalom came up. Our delegation and the Gesher L'Shalom women fell in love with each other. We were up late talking, exchanging ideas, and learning about each other. We got cold drinks for everybody from a machine in the hotel because they stayed so long that we ran out of refreshments! It was a wonderful surprise. Some years later, they became the Israeli section of WILPF.

One emotional part of the trip was our visit to Yad Vashem outside of Jerusalem. It was a memorial for the 6 million Jews who were killed by the Nazis. We also visited the Garden of the Righteous, where plants and trees memorialized non-Jews who had died in support of Jews or who had heroically saved the lives of Jews. It includes trees for the people who fed Anne Frank's family and religious leaders who risked or lost their lives to hide Jews.

A sign on the grounds of the memorial warned, "Beware of Suspicious Objects." It was demoralizing to see that such a sign was needed at the memorial.

On our last day in Israel, we headed to the airport only to learn that the Israeli pilots were on strike! No planes were leaving. We'd experienced so many challenges on our trip that when I told everyone, their only response was to burst out laughing.

Eventually we were able to get a plane to Naples. From there I had to find sixteen seats on a plane going to the U.S. We didn't have any reservations since we had planned to travel home on a different flight. Naples wasn't far from Israel and many other passengers were pushing to get to the ticket counter. I kept moving through the crowd toward the desk saying, "Excuse me. Excuse me."

The ticket clerk was so impressed with my politeness that she took me first. We got our sixteen seats on the flight home. Some WILPF members had notified the media about our return, so when we finally arrived back at JFK airport, representatives from two newspapers were waiting to meet us: *The People's Daily World* (the U.S. Communist paper) and the New York *Daily News*. The representative of *The People's Daily World* had flowers for me!

It was quite ironic that it was those two papers who responded to the press notices; *they couldn't have been more different from each other!* The other delegation members had to scramble to catch their planes home but since JFK was my final stop, I spoke with the media myself.

Mort also met me at JFK, and we drove home together. While I was thrilled to see my family again, the evening was somewhat of a letdown after all the weeks of excitement.

Our trip made it clear how much more complicated the situation in the Middle East was than a conflict between Arabs and Jews. This simplistic analysis was presented and maintained by the media and most government sources. Being pro-Israeli meant you supported everything Israel was doing, and you opposed Palestinian independence. Being pro-Arab meant you were against the existence of the State of Israel, anti-Semitic, and in favor of terrorism. The situation was, and still is, much more complex than that.

Our trip enabled us to see for ourselves what was happening in the Middle East. Lebanon was almost destroyed by wars. The arms race was impoverishing both Israel and Egypt; and it was beginning to affect Syria as well. No country had secure borders. Millions were displaced as they fled the conflicts, creating continual instability. The conditions were degrading for people living under occupation as well as for the occupiers. While a conservative alliance grew between the U.S., Saudi Arabia, Iran, Israel, and Egypt; the peace movement lacked unity. Meanwhile Egypt was suppressing both international and domestic peace organizations.

The delegation summarized our observations in a report excerpted here: "We were encouraged by the [Jewish] Israelis we met who advocated recognition of the self-determination of the Palestinians. However, the recent Palestinian raids into Israel hardened the right-wing there and we didn't see it as constructive. We were encouraged by most of the Arab leaders, including spokespersons of the PLO who accept the reality of the Israeli state and the belief Palestinians must find ways to live in peace with Israel. They do, however, believe progress in this direction is reliant on Israeli recognition of the Palestinians' right to a state of their own. Some of us are terribly disappointed that the faction of the PLO favoring negotiation has been rebuffed by Israel often enough that the faction favoring military intervention has gained ascendancy. We believe the only chance for progress is comprehensive peace talks with all parties of the conflict included."

Even today, this report could be considered controversial.

When WILPF had a table at the National Education Association meeting in Atlantic City, two men in suits walked up to us and said accusingly, "What are you doing here? How did you get in here?"

We could have been asked the same question about our delegation to the Middle East. Who were we to travel to these countries, meeting with government and NGO leaders? We were not elected officials. We were not government leaders or hired consultants. *Who were we?*

We were a group of individuals who decided to do what we could. In 1919, another group of WILPF delegates traveled to Versailles with four resolutions for a just and lasting peace following World War I. Like them, we were WILPF delegates on a mission to learn so we could better act for peace and justice in the Middle East. We shared information and ideas that might build bridges between conflicting sides.

Speaking and Writing on Middle East Peace

Just about every member of the delegation fulfilled her obligation. We were all involved in speaking and writing. We promoted a solution of comprehensive peace talks that included all parties to the conflict. We could make no guarantee that such negotiations would bring peace, but we had seen the alternative.

Soon after our return in 1978, the local Westchester County WILPF branch sponsored a meeting where I reported on our trip. The auditorium was large, but it was crowded with people. We were pioneers, and people were eager to hear about our experiences.

I also spoke on panels with other Middle East peace and justice leaders. You may remember Allan Solomonow, who introduced me to my first PLO member several years back. Allan was instrumental in helping me develop an understanding of the region and what was going on there. He was also instrumental in breaking silence on Middle East issues.

Members of the U.S. peace movement rarely included broader Middle East issues in their visions, focusing almost exclusively on Israel and the Arabs. Allan found ways to challenge those omissions. He was one of the very first American Jewish activists to do so. He advocated for mutual recognition, dialogue between Israel and the PLO, commitment to non-violence, compromise, a two-state solution, and a nuclear-free Middle East. He was even in touch with Palestinians, a rarity for U.S. activists.

In 1970, Allan, together with several other Jewish intellectuals, activists, and academics, founded CONAME, Committee for New Alternatives in the Middle East. This was the first American organization to focus attention on non-violent solutions between Israel and the Palestinians.

While working on staff with the Fellowship of Reconciliation, Allan organized a panel for a major meeting at the Church Center for the United Nations (CCUN) in New York. An assortment of Middle East peace groups was involved in the meeting, and it promised to be an informative and engaging event.

I looked at the panel he'd arranged, and I said, "Allan, those are all men."

And Allan, while looking right at my face, sincerely said, "I don't know any women who could be on the panel." *He said this to my face!*

We had worked together for years on Middle East peace and justice, he knew about my work with WILPF, yet it had not occurred to him to invite me—or any other women working on this topic—to speak on the panel.

It was hard to speak up, but when I did Allan agreed to include me on the panel. It was one of my best speeches. He also learned from the experience and became much more sensitive over the years.

I was on another panel discussion on the Middle East in Philadelphia at the University of Pennsylvania in 1987. I was nervous because I was speaking outside of a WILPF audience. I met up with local WILPF members for supper before the event began. I was grateful to have the WILPF women in the audience to support me. I really needed them, as you shall see.

Rabbi Arthur Waskow was the moderator. He was a friend of mine whom I respected. He wrote *The Freedom*

Seder and eventually became a well-known progressive speaker and activist. *The Freedom Seder* was a groundbreaking Passover Haggadah that drew parallels between the histories of oppression and resistance of the Black and Jewish peoples.

Also on the program were two other male speakers, including one Arab. The plan called for Art to open up a discussion before the panelists spoke and then take questions from the audience.

I'd worked hard preparing my talk and was anxious about how it would be received. When our speeches were over, Art did not take questions from the audience as planned. Instead, he spoke in response to the talks presented by the men on the panel. He only responded to what the *men* said. His remarks left no time for questions or discussion from the audience, nor did he mention anything I had said. I was completely ignored. It was an awful feeling. I assumed my presentation must have been horrible to be ignored that way.

When it was over, the three men huddled together on stage and left me sitting there alone. The WILPF women came up on stage and surrounded me with praise and support. They said what a great job I did and how proud they were. Thank goodness for them.

The following Sunday, back home I was reading the *New York Times* and saw a book review by Rabbi Arthur Waskow on the topic of Jewish life. He'd written that although the book was very good, it ignored Jewish women and their unique contributions and struggles. What irony. I wrote to Art and told him what I thought—he and the other men had ignored me after my presentation, and it had felt horrible.

Art wrote back and explained that he didn't say anything about my talk because he had agreed with everything I said. While his response was complimentary of my presentation, it did not change the experience of being ignored during the post-panel discussion. I did notice and appreciate that Art became more sensitive in the future. And I was determined to be engaged in future discussions, with or without any moderator's support.

I continued to speak and write on the Middle East for many years. As an example, in 2011, members of the National WILPF Middle East Committee began work on an educational booklet: *Hamas at the Middle East Peace Table: Why?* The booklet was authored by Barbara Taft and Ellen Rosser. Tura Campanella Cook, Barbara Nielsen, and I made up the editorial committee. The purpose of this booklet—like much of our work on the Middle East—was to provide a more nuanced explanation of what was happening than people could read in mainstream media.

In January 2006, Hamas won more seats in the Palestinian legislative election than any other party—partially based on their ability to improve public services, but also in response to corruption within the existing Fatah government. Because the U.S. had labeled Hamas a terrorist group, they were excluded from participating in peace negotiations, which meant that not all relevant parties were represented. We did not deny that Israel and Hamas were enemies, but to achieve peace, it is necessary to speak with one's enemies. The booklet was an important contribution to understanding the history of Hamas and illustrating how U.S. policy shaped a narrative to support its own objectives—as it continues to do today.

On October 7, 2023, nearly 18 years after the last Palestinian election, Hamas launched an attack on Israel, killing hundreds of people and taking 250 hostages. By February 2024, the Israeli army had killed tens of thousands of Palestinians, destroying cities and infrastructure. Yet some Israelis and Palestinians still work together to develop a path to peace that is not based on military dominance. By seeking to understand the people involved—rather than relying on oversimplified representations—we can support these efforts and advocate policies that encourage a just peace.

•

Things have changed drastically since I started to speak publicly and write about the Middle East. In the past, I would start off saying, "I had this picture of chalutzim, who were Jewish Israeli pioneers . . . they were the heroes; young white men who wore white open-necked shirts and everyone working together on kibbutzim. With this stereotype, it seems impossible these men could do anything wrong to Arabs . . ."

I used this image to resonate with many American Jews (and others) who were familiar with the kibbutzim communities before I would go on to discuss Palestinian rights. Into my early thirties, I thought a lot like these other young American Jews: the priority was establishing an Israeli State for Jews to be safe. By the time I started speaking, I had a very different view of the Israel-Palestine situation. I had traveled there myself and seen the horrors of the refugee camps, the conflicted feelings of Israeli officials on the situation, and the uncertainty within Israel. I knew it was more complicated than my audience realized, and I needed them to see that.

Since those early days, much has changed. The situation on the ground in Israel and occupied areas such as Gaza remains awful. No matter how you look at it, occupation cannot be anything but brutal. The money and forces behind Islamophobia and anti-Semitism are still alive and thriving. However, we have seen new and positive developments in the struggle for a just peace.

For one, Arab and Palestinian groups have formed and become more vocal in the U.S. Organizations such as The Council on American-Islamic Relations (CAIR); U.S. Campaign for Palestinian Rights; and Students for Justice in Palestine have created a voice for Palestinians and Muslims in this country. Attacks on academic freedom for those who speak out are being met with protests, and sometimes success. In the past, when a Palestinian would talk to me about the awful situation in the Middle East, I would say, "Write a letter to the paper. Talk to your Congressperson."

The reply would be, "Once they see my Arab name, they shut me down and dismiss my concerns."

Now discussions are more possible, although pro-Palestinian activists and their allies are still harassed and threatened. College groups like "Students for Justice in Palestine" are particularly targeted.

As the generations who lived through the Holocaust pass away, its tragedies begin to fade in people's memories. The driving passion for a safe haven for Jews in Israel has lessened as the horrors of the Holocaust move further into history. Courageous Jewish Israeli voices are starting to join Palestinian voices in their call for lasting change and peace.

Young Jewish groups have also developed in the U.S. and become effective in ways we never dreamed of in the '70s and '80s. Jewish groups, like Breira, attempted to oppose U.S. policy on Israel in the past, but the time wasn't ripe for their success. Now we have a very successful national group called Jewish Voice for Peace; a young activist group, If Not Now; the centrist group, J Street; JOOT (Jews on Our Own Terms); and more.

We have also seen a growing understanding of the intersectionality of issues. For example, a demonstration sign that says, "NO WALLS ON OUR BORDER OR IN PALESTINE," referring to a wall between Mexico and the U.S. and between Palestine and Israel. The two situations are no longer isolated; even developing into discussion on how we treat refugees and what their rights should be. I have been inspired over and over again by the work today's peace and justice activists are doing, frequently led by young Black and brown women.

Part 4

Leading WILPF and Beyond

WILPF-US Executive Director

I did peace and justice work with WILPF-US for many years; volunteering in different cities where we lived and participating in local, state, national, and international events.

After the Middle East Peace Delegation, the most significant event I helped to organize was the 21st WILPF Triennial International Congress in August 1980. It was held at Quinnipiac College outside New Haven, Connecticut.

We had over two hundred participants who joined in a variety of workshops, such as "Ending the Arms Race" and "Human Rights and National Liberation,"[1] led by representatives from different countries. I was determined to have a more diverse International Congress than in the past, when the U.S. and other Western countries were the only ones featured. In retrospect, I think we made some progress, but not nearly enough.

In addition to the workshops, we had an International Peace Gift Shop, folk music performances, training in non-

---

1 The complete list of topics is as follows: Ending the Arms Race; Arms Trade; Women and the Military; European Security and Its Implications for World Peace; Achieving Conversion with Full Employment; Western Economies and Their Impact on Developing Countries; Use and Control of Natural Resources; Energy; Racism: the Great Divider; Human Rights and National Liberation; and Education for Peace and Freedom.

violence, and a massive rally held at Yale attended by over eight hundred people who heard remarks by delegates from the Philippines, Cuba and Vietnam, among others.

The WILPFul Singers (Libby is second from the right), 1980

The Congress concluded with a 65th birthday gala. At the end of the conference, the WILPFul singers—as was the custom—wrote and performed an original song. Along with Margaret Stein, I usually helped write lyrics. Together, we were known as "FranknStein." Our music was always a big hit and we loved how music brought the whole group together. With the expert and enthusiastic work of the New Haven WILPF branch and the U.S. staff, we held a terrific event.

When it was over, Mort and I happily got in our car and drove to Maine for a well-deserved vacation. After visiting Portland, Maine years earlier, I fell in love with the state; particularly the 365 "Calendar Islands" surrounding the mainland. Our family vacationed for years on one of them: Peaks Island.

•

By the time I had applied for the job of Executive Director, I had been volunteering with WILPF-US for 20 years; on the Childhood Education Committee in the 1960s and on the WILPF Middle East Committee in the 1970s. I was known as a leader, and I was excited at the possibility of helping lead the U.S. section.

I had interviews with the Personnel Committee and staff, followed by a private interview with WILPF icon, Mildred Scott Olmstead. She had been the National Director from 1934 until 1966. She asked if I was a pacifist because all of the previous directors had been. I told her that I didn't believe wars and violence could solve today's problems. She said, "Close enough."

I got the job and in 1981 our family moved from White Plains, NY to Philadelphia, where WILPF national headquarters was then located. For the first few years I thrived in the position. I was energized by the work and our wonderful staff.

My first major project as Executive Director was to organize a seminar that was part of a series by U.S. WILPF and the Soviet Women's Committee. The locations alternated between the U.S. and the Soviet Union. The previous Executive Director had been involved in scheduling the date of the upcoming seminar in the U.S, but no specific plans had been made for the agenda, U.S. attendance, local support, or meals. Although not much had been done to prepare for it, I believed in the idea heartily, so I threw myself into the work with enthusiasm.

Our generous host for the seminar was Bryn Mawr

College, located in a suburb of Philadelphia. After the seminar, our Soviet guests and a group of the WILPF-US participants got together to socialize before our Soviet guests departed. I had ordered a cake with "Mir y Druzhba" (Peace and Friendship) written on it. The Soviet visitors had brought vodka.

We toasted both each other and peace over and over, lustily singing out melodies between toasts. One of the visitors was a journalist and a true Bolshevik (Communist revolutionary)—we had met previously in the Soviet Union. She commented, "Libby isn't really interested in the toast. It's a good excuse to have a drink of vodka!"

We all laughed, sang, danced—or more accurately, swayed— ate the cake, and drank vodka.

Our relationship with the Soviet Women's Committee, among other activities, prompted suspicion during the Cold War. In October 1982, WILPF, Women Strike for Peace (WSP), and one other women's group, Peace Links, were accused in the *Washington Post* of being Soviet fronts. I wrote an emergency notice to members urging letters to the editor to correct this mistake. Many members took action, but what really saved us was a number of male Congress members standing up and declaring that their *wives* were members in some of these organizations and were loyal Americans. Their public support of their wives helped us refute the attack. *The Post* actually retracted its story. It was a groundbreaking moment. I traveled to Washington with flowers to support our D.C. staff who dealt with the brunt of the attack.

Mort supported me in my peace work: helping organize events, dropping me off for protests, and keeping watch over our kids while I was away. But Mort was also personally passionate about peace. He initiated—and was the chief organizer of—the "October Witness of 1983," which he still considers the single most important accomplishment of his life. It was a rally in Philadelphia on the steps of the Art Museum against sending nuclear-tipped Pershing II and Cruise Missiles to West Germany. Opposing those weapon systems was also a major campaign of WILPF US, but Mort organized the event with a variety of groups.

Months before the rally, Mort wrote, ". . . My primary concern is not Philadelphia or the history of early German settlement in Philadelphia, but the need to bring the special importance of the Pershing II missiles and their deployment in West Germany before a wide public . . ."

Mort had learned that a year-long public relations campaign was planned to set the stage for West German acceptance of the missiles. The U.S. and the West German government combined the celebration of the founding of Germantown (part of Philadelphia) with news of the missiles' deployment in central Europe[2]. This PR maneuver exploited the long "friendship" between Germany and the U.S., while ignoring the fact that those first Germans were religious pacifists, predominantly Quakers and Mennonites. The event's slogan, "Friendship Without Missiles," drew attention to this fact.

At Mort's suggestion, important peace leaders in West Germany were invited to speak at the demonstration. We were surprised by their quick and positive responses, which also showed the seriousness of the planned deployment in the eyes of many Germans.

Prior to the main event, I attended a joint worship service of Quakers and Mennonites, then joined hundreds of people walking to the Museum. Mort wrote, "At twilight, I saw two columns of Quakers and Mennonites [and other activists] bearing lighted candles walking in slow procession from the worship to the demonstration site. I was overwhelmed by emotion. 'I did this?' I thought to myself. 'How did an atheist Jewish radical do this?' I was proud."

---

2 Germantown was founded 300 years earlier, on Oct. 6th, 1683, by the first Germans to reach the New World.

To our knowledge, it was the largest peace demonstration in Philadelphia history until the Black Lives Matter demonstration in June 2020. Our protest gathered 20,000 people at the Philadelphia Museum of Art.

The following year, in 1984, the group Promoting Enduring Peace invited Mort and me to speak during a two-week cruise up the Volga River in the Soviet Union. I was invited based on my work as Executive Director of U.S. WILPF, and Mort was invited based on his role organizing the October Witness of 1983.

Promoting Enduring Peace was one of many groups encouraging relationships between Americans and Soviets. We needed to challenge the Cold War rhetoric in the U.S. and the demonization of Soviet people. The cruise included U.S. and Soviet passengers with an agenda full of activities: workshops, social events, and visiting significant sites. We talked to Soviet peace activists, journalists, and everyday citizens about relations between the U.S. and the USSR.

About a dozen male Soviet experts were onboard to help with the Soviet perspective on the topics. No women were included in the Soviet delegation. I asked them why and the men responded by saying, "They're busy."

It was a very unsatisfying answer and reminded me of the same answer the Syrian Jewish men had given me on my trip to the Middle East in 1978.

The onboard workshops fell under four main topics: U.S.-Soviet Relations; News, Media, and the Peace Movement; the United Nations; and American and Soviet Lifestyles. Mort had become well-versed in the politics of U.S. arms and was invited to speak about "The Military Dimension." I was one of the discussion leaders on "News, Media, and the Peace Movement."

We actually had difficulty with the media during part of the trip, highlighting one reason tensions between the U.S. and Soviet Union were so bad. We called a press conference before we left the country, explaining how peace and connection were our goals. Instead, the media turned it into an attack on us.

They asked, "In a war, which side would you be more comfortable being on?"

It was a question more in line with the McCarthyite era of the 1950s than 1984. They asked a lot of hostile questions and then never reported on the trip. I guess they didn't see it as a story because we didn't condemn the Soviet system. Afterwards our Soviet hosts said to us, "You have courage!"

We had also invited the U.S. media to cover a peace demonstration on July 3 in Volgograd, but of course they didn't.

All of the Soviet peace activists were part of the Soviet Peace Committee, which was approved by the government. We had some difficulty understanding how each other's peace movements functioned. We asked the Soviets, "Why only one big organization?"

They replied with, "Why do you need more than one?"

They didn't see the need for all the different organizations we have. Our peace movement appeared fragmented to them, and in some ways, I saw their point.

We stopped in a few cities along the river: Volgograd (which used to be Stalingrad) and Ulyanovsk (the birthplace of Lenin) among others. We spent ten days visiting Moscow, Kiev, and Leningrad. In almost every city, we met with the local branch of the Soviet Peace Committee. In Moscow, I met with the Soviet Women's Committee, and Mort and I both met with the head of the Institute on U.S./Canada Studies. In a couple of cities, we visited the local Friendship House, which was a cultural exchange center for foreign visitors.

One revelation that stood out from the cruise was the pure devastation on the Soviet Union wrought by WWII. Twenty million people died, and the losses were still evident. In the cemeteries, you could see brides and grooms on their wedding day placing flowers on the graves of lost loved ones. They were very proud of what they'd managed to build in the forty years since the war and were also afraid of it being destroyed again.

We visited a Soviet memorial statue located in a large, beautiful park. We'd entered quietly and respectfully, but we were surprised when we noticed young children running around and laughing. It struck me as inappropriate for a memorial. When I asked one of the parents about it, she answered that the freedom of the children to play was why the adults had fought in the first place, so their laughter wasn't disrespectful but rather a rewarding result.

We were still on the cruise for the 4th of July, so I organized a celebration that included a reading of the Declaration of Independence and a square dance. The Soviets showed a lot of respect for our holiday. We found it more meaningful, too, reflecting on the meaning of the day without the distractions of hot dogs and fireworks.

After the cruise, eighty participants got together to raise funds to place an ad in the *New York Times* and share some of the feelings inspired by the trip. We hoped the ad would help change Americans' perceptions of the Soviet Union.

●

WILPF is a multi-issue organization, so my work as ED spanned a variety of areas. One of the major projects during my tenure as ED was the STAR Campaign. It was initiated by Naomi Marcus in 1982, who was chairman [sic] of the Program Committee at the time. STAR was an acronym for "Stop the Arms Race." Staff and volunteers, working with the National Program Committee prepared material for local branches across the country. We had a Literature Department on the basement level of 2013 Race Street, Philadelphia, which was our headquarters for many years.

We were fortunate to have Joanne Woodward, a famous movie actress (and Paul Newman's wife), come and speak at one of our large meetings. She was the star of our STAR campaign. It was quite exciting. Two of our young staff members drove to New York to meet with her ahead of time to make arrangements. Before Joanne talked with them, her husband called her in to another room and whispered for her to, "Be careful with those women!"

It was a failed attempt at a whisper because our staff easily overheard him. Instead of being offended, they found it funny. Progressive ideas intimidate many people, famous or not.

I was also involved in a number of national coalitions. I traveled often to New York and D.C. to participate in all sorts of meetings. Some mornings, arriving in Philadelphia's 30th Street train station, a cardboard cup of coffee in one hand and my briefcase in the other, I had to check my calendar to see which city I was going to that day.

My main speaking and writing themes were U.S. policy; the intersection of Peace and Freedom; and successful WILPF projects. Most of my talks were to WILPF audiences, but several were at churches or Quaker meeting houses. I spoke at a church in Montreal and a small house in Portland, Maine.

My schedule kept me constantly moving, always presenting or engaging people in discussion. At one point I was invited to Germany where I spoke to a small group in Bremen, then ten thousand people outside a U.S. Army base in West Germany, and to fifty thousand people in Cologne who cheered when I was introduced as a member of U.S. WILPF. I believe they were cheering for the U.S. peace movement. The day after I came home from Germany, I went back into the WILPF office to work. Then the next day, I flew to Berkeley, California to participate in WILPF Middle East Committee discussions.

After a productive day of Middle East Committee meetings, we went out to dinner where I ate spicy food and drank wine. Feeling somewhat dizzy and needing air, I went outside; and then I fainted. It had never happened before and hasn't happened since, but I'd been running around and dealing with several time changes in quick succession. Fortunately, I was staying with Dolores Taller and her husband, Steve Taller, who was a physician. He made sure I rested at their home and recuperated well. The guest room where I stayed had a full library of mysteries. I was quite content there. Unfortunately, I had to cancel a series of talks I was scheduled to make across California.

Reuben getting his diploma from the President of the University after Libby spoke at Ohio Wesleyan University commencement, 1982

One of my most memorable speeches was for my son Reuben's commencement ceremony at Ohio Wesleyan University. After working on the school newspaper in high school, Reuben became the editor as a junior, which was a great honor. Reuben was conducting an interview of the university chaplain for the paper when he noticed a poster on the chaplain's wall. It read, "It will be a Great Day when the schools get all of the money they need and the Air Force has to hold a bake sale to buy a bomber."

Reuben exclaimed, "That's my mother's poster!"

Reuben talked to the chaplain about the WILPF poster and my work as the Executive Director. That's how I came to speak at the school and eventually became the commencement speaker at Reuben's graduation in 1982.

The students gathered monthly during the school year to hear speakers in a large auditorium. With the support of Reuben and the chaplain (and my famous poster), I was invited to speak at one of the monthly student gatherings. The usual topics were along the lines of "What I did on my summer vacation." This was right around the time that the U.S. was planning to send Pershing and Cruise missiles to Germany—and that was the topic of my speech. My talk was entitled "Visit Europe Before It's Too Late." I brought pounds and pounds of literature about the missiles and about WILPF. Reuben had a radio program on campus and used it to advertise my visit to campus. At the end of one show, he dropped his professionalism and said, "Come on and hear my mom speak."

Well, it worked; many students did come to hear "Reuben's mom." I'd placed the literature on the front of the stage and after my talk it was gobbled up. The successful talk made me a candidate for commencement speaker. The university liked to choose a graduate's relative to be the speaker. The previous speaker was William Webster, past head of the FBI, who was the uncle of a graduate—I had a very different perspective!

I received a letter from the head of the class inviting me to speak, and of course I accepted. Then I got a follow-up letter from an official of the college reminding me to be careful how I spoke because not everyone would agree with me. After so many years working for peace and justice, I was used to people not agreeing with me!

I needed to be on campus a day before the event. The college put me up in a nice private room on campus and invited me to have breakfast with the Dean, the chaplain, and many others. The evening before the ceremony, Reuben had arranged a lovely place for dinner with several of his friends, as well as his brother Alan and me. It was a lot of fun. Unfortunately, Mort couldn't be there because he was staying in Cleveland overnight in order to bring my father to the commencement the next day. They arrived at the college very early on the morning of commencement and were able to join us at the table for breakfast. My dad put on his yarmulke and conversed warmly with the chaplain. He was treated with honor, and I was very happy to share the moment with him. I can still picture my father at the breakfast, drinking a cup of coffee and engaging with everyone.

A big disarmament demonstration took place in New York a day before the commencement. Mort had organized buses from Philadelphia to go to the protest but couldn't go himself because he and my dad were going to the commencement. A number of women wearing peace buttons on their graduation caps recognized me, grinned, and waved to me as they were in line on their way to the ceremony. They had clearly gone to the demonstration and come back in time to graduate.

It was time for the commencement speech. After addressing all members of the audience, I continued as follows:

> I always try to think of something funny with which to start my talks—I hardly ever succeed. Nothing funny every happens to me on my way to the speaker's platform. But I must admit I read the comics and just two weeks ago saw my prepared commencement

speech brilliantly lampooned in Doonesbury. So, I had to start preparing <u>my</u> talk all over again.

I read every newspaper report on commencement addresses I could find, from Doonesbury to Alan Alda to the Presidents of colleges throughout the country. One theme emerges over and again—and almost anyone you invited to speak would have said the same thing: *The drive to war must be stopped.*

I add my own themes:

- There is no such thing as a limited nuclear war

- Even the <u>threat</u> of war is depriving you of your fair share of the future –

- We can change the direction of our country

- It is possible to create the most productive, most satisfying society the world has ever known.

I went on to describe in more detail how the threat of war impacted their dreams—and the incredible possibilities available through international cooperation. I invited the graduates not to replace their parents' generation in making the world better, but to join us. The conclusion of my talk included a reference to a Hebrew verse, followed by the English translation:

I call heaven and earth to witness against you this day, that I have set before thee life and death, the blessing and the curse: therefore,

> choose life, that thou mayest live, thou and
> thy seed. (Deut. 30:19)

After the ceremony was over, I went down to join my family and an old dear friend Dorothy Blackman. My dad said with awe, "You spoke Hebrew in front of all those people!"

That's why I did it, for my father.

•

As my time in the Executive Director role continued, I experienced one of the biggest challenges of my career. Barbara Armentrout, our full-time editor of the monthly WILPF national magazine, *Peace and Freedom*, was excellent. She had an incredible notebook outlining how to develop and publish the magazine. She consulted with the Advisory Committee before each issue went to print. I thought she'd be with us forever. Unfortunately, Barbara moved on and we had to hire a new editor.

We advertised the position and had lots of applicants. It took a while, but we finally hired one of the candidates, a Black woman. I gave Barbara's notebook to the new editor and told her to use the info in it until she knew her way around. Then she could start using her own methods. For a couple of weeks, I made an effort to visit her office every morning to see if she needed any help or had any questions.

As the time approached for the next National Board Meeting, I asked each staff member to submit a report about the work they'd completed since the previous meeting. In the past, the Executive Director would combine all the reports from the staff and make one report to the board. However, the new editor alone among the staff refused to turn in a report. No matter what I said, she insisted that she would give her own report to the Board, which she did.

In her report, she accused me of not trusting her, because

I went to her office every morning. She thought I was worried about her arriving on time! I really wanted her to succeed and that's why I was checking in with her regularly; not because I didn't trust her. I saw it as checking *in*, not checking *on*.

While we had some difficult discussions at the board meeting it was clear to most board members that my actions were taken in good faith, and there were no immediate repercussions.

After the board meeting, I found that the editor was not living up to the job description. She wasn't consulting with the Advisory Committee, following the previous editor's manual, or meeting deadlines for the publication. Our staff contracts provided a process for letting people know when they were not meeting the job requirements and giving them an opportunity to improve. Following this process, I told the editor that she needed to follow the job description in order to keep the job and gave her a period of time to make improvements. All of this was done in cooperation with the Personnel Committee. My warning didn't work. The editor refused to make the changes and didn't meet the job demands. I had to fire her.

The editor immediately went to a Philadelphia civil rights agency and charged WILPF with racial discrimination and wrongful termination! The ex-editor claimed that I harassed her and then fired her because she was Black. She wanted WILPF to make a payment to compensate her for her suffering.

The staff was behind me; they were happy when I first hired her, but they'd seen the editor not live up to her contract and my efforts to redirect her. Our bookkeeper, our front desk manager, and a senior office assistant were all Black women, so when the representatives from the civil rights agency visited our office, they were greeted by these respected Black women.

We called in our lawyer on retainer, Alice Ballard, who was from a very well-known Philadelphia family and terrific at her job. Ultimately, the board decided to pay the ex-editor what she asked. They wanted to avoid having WILPF publicly charged with being racist. When they finally offered her the amount she requested, she came back and asked for more because she said we had "wasted her time." Reluctantly, they decided to pay it.

Looking back about forty years, I can now understand her perceptions. Perhaps I could have handled it differently; I reacted to what she said rather than what she might have been feeling. It was a frustrating and difficult ordeal.

My greatest challenges were still to come. It became clear that certain staff and board members wanted me out of the Executive Director role. They floated rumors that I was not a good administrator, but no one offered any feedback or suggestions on what I should do differently. I started to question my contributions and ability to do the job.

It was Mort who helped me realize it was not really about my administration skills. I'll never know the real issue behind their agenda. Maybe it was my politics, or I wasn't feminist enough, or even just too old. In any case, the board began to take action against me.

They hired a consultant to observe me and make recommendations. She gave me two pieces of advice; one was to stop holding my hands over my head when I was thinking because it looked unprofessional. The second piece of advice was even more ridiculous: I often made and served coffee in my large office because we held frequent meetings there. She disliked this ritual and felt that I should only prep coffee in the downstairs staff kitchen. Neither recommendation would have made anyone a better administrator.

After the consultant submitted her report, the Board President, Anne Ivey, organized a retreat. She called an executive meeting and told me that since I was staff, I couldn't attend. It felt like a betrayal considering that I had been the one who encouraged her to run for the position of President. Fortunately, one of my supporters, Anne Nelson, knew the bylaws and showed them to Anne. It said the Executive Director was a member of the Executive Committee, so I sat in on the meeting. It did not go well.

In the past, the Program Committee, composed of paid program staff and active volunteers, decided on the national program. Then once the program priorities were decided, the staff and I would create a work plan to support them. During this meeting, I was told to prepare a work plan for U.S. WILPF Section—without having the national program decided. I couldn't even think how to respond. I just froze.

We moved on to the next topic, which was WILPF's financial problems. Raising funds was a priority. I offered to prioritize my time on raising money and was told not to do it. They did not want me to work on raising needed funds.

The board no longer wanted me to do my job as Executive Director. Although I resigned from the job in 1986, it was not my own choice. I applied for unemployment compensation since I had been pressured to resign by a hostile work environment. The board disputed my application and I never received unemployment compensation, or any type of severance pay. While I was Executive Director, I had approved unemployment compensation for everyone who left, no matter the reason. I was really down and depressed. My confidence was badly injured for a long time after that.

One bright spot was that Promoting Enduring Peace again invited me to speak on a Peace Cruise in 1986, even though I had resigned from WILPF. This time it was sailing down the Mississippi River with a delegation from the Soviet Union joining our U.S. group. It was a great opportunity to immerse myself in peace work rather than dwelling on what had happened.

We stopped at several cities along the Mississippi River, surprised to be greeted by enthusiastic crowds everywhere. Keep in mind this was in the midst of the Cold War.

The locals were also surprised as they saw us walking off

the boat. They commented, "Wow, they look like us. You can't tell the difference between the Russians and the Americans!"

It was a great feeling to see the impact we had on people's attitudes toward the Soviets.

Several months after my resignation, I got a call from the Chairperson of the local Philadelphia WILPF branch. Mort answered the phone and passed it over to me. I didn't want to take it—I was mad at everyone in WILPF—but I did answer. The Chairperson told me the branch wanted to present the annual Peace Dove award to me at the branch luncheon. In those days, a hundred or more people would attend the luncheons. I said I would accept the award if I could speak. It was agreed.

On the day of the award ceremony, I started by saying: "I didn't get this award for keeping my mouth shut and I'm not going to start now." I spoke about what WILPF *should* be doing politically in contrast to what they *were* doing. I got a standing ovation. The award meant a lot to me, and the response to my talk helped me start gaining back my self-confidence.

A Career in Peace Work Concluded

Before long, Ethel Taylor, a local Philadelphia activist and a long-time leader of Women Strike for Peace (WSP), recruited me to their organization. Ethel and others (notably Bella Abzug and Dagmar Wilson) planted the seed for WSP at a WILPF national meeting in the early 1960s. They wanted to concentrate on dangerous nuclear weapons fallout. Researchers found Strontium-90, a radioactive metal, in breastmilk which was having a harmful effect on baby's teeth. Ethel, Bella, Dagmar, and many others wanted WILPF to concentrate on the physical effects on babies of these ghastly weapons. The rest of WILPF wanted to focus on the bigger picture of war and injustice.

What resulted was the birth of a new organization, Women Strike for Peace. They started with a big protest in 1961, with fifty thousand women marching in sixty U.S. cities against the testing of nuclear weapons by both the U.S. and the Soviet Union.

I stuck with WILPF because I really believed in a multi-issue organization, where the intersectionality of issues was considered. Over time, WSP's concerns broadened to focus on ending nuclear-proliferation and U.S. involvement in wars. WSP also played a critical part in helping end the House Un-American Activities Committee—later renamed the Committee on Internal Security—which investigated private citizens and organizations for Communist ties. I was delighted when Ethel called and offered me the job of Fundraiser.

I had plenty of experience fundraising and was always looking for creative ways to support our peace work. On the Soviet Peace Cruise, I'd met a U.S. businessman who clearly had a lot of money. He told me he liked my kind of feminism and seemed to resonate with what I had to say. Back at the WSP office, I wrote him a letter reminding him of who I was and asking for a contribution. I received a letter from his secretary saying he didn't have any idea who I was.

Not to be deterred, I sent back the letter and instead of a return address on the envelope, I glued on a photo of myself! He then remembered me and made a generous contribution to keep our peace work moving. I told this story at a fundraising workshop years later and the person who led the workshop said she told the story many times afterwards.

One great idea that never happened was to have a special fundraising luncheon prepared by men. We were going to call it "Men who Cook for Women who Strike for Peace." I called several activist men I knew, and they all had a special dish they were willing to prepare. I had even begun a song, "Give me some men who are stouthearted men who will cook for the ones they adore . . ."

It was a take-off on a call to the troops, sung by Nelson Eddy, motion picture star. I had this picture in my mind of the men entering the hall wearing chef hats and carrying their special dish, and we'd all be singing. Ethel called together our supporters and our office was packed. We presented the idea and asked for members to help set it up, but no one volunteered. The idea went down the drain, which was a shame because it was such a good idea.

Ethel Taylor was the National Coordinator of WSP, but in January 1987 I became the full-time Executive Director. Ethel remained active and continued to sustain us financially. Philadelphia became the site of the WSP national office, although it was in a somewhat decrepit building on 13th Street, which was not an attractive location. We were up on the 5th floor and the elevator only worked every other day. We finally moved to a nicer building at 19th and Chestnut.

Waiting for consensus with WSP (Libby far left), mid-1980's

Ending U.S. involvement in wars and military culture remained the priority at WSP. We had wonderful activists who were young, creative, energetic, and cooperative. I was new at WSP. One time we went to a national peace demonstration in D.C. with this big banner that took ten of us across to hold it. We went to the Lincoln Memorial and stood up on the top steps. All the other demonstrators were down below. We figured we weren't supposed to be on the steps since no other activists were there, but we decided to stay as long as we could.

I was holding up one end of the banner and a cop came up to me and said, "You're gonna have to get down."

And I said, "I can't make the decision by myself; we need to have consensus."

I had caught on to WSP culture: get away with as much as you can!

Consensus takes a long time. Eventually we had to leave, but in the meantime, more people were able to see us up there with our banner.

Another project involved creating a major campaign against the U.S. Strategic Defense Initiative (SDI) to arm the skies. We created a tape using the studio of a liberal radio station in Philadelphia. Our tape ended up being created and spoken by women, which was unusual for the times. I worked with wonderful volunteers, particularly, two young women who researched and produced a brochure to accompany the tape. I sent copies to a few significant activists and asked organizations to support our efforts. We sold a lot of tapes and got endorsements from several well-known people.

We also dreamed up a great project which unfortunately never came to fruition. George H.W. Bush was President at the time, and he had used the phrase "a thousand points of light" referring to volunteers across the country. We wanted him to sign specific peace legislation and our idea was to get our supporters and members to send "a thousand points of pencils" to show their support for the legislation. We found out that we couldn't send pencils in the mail and scratched the idea, but I still loved the poetic nature of it. It was one of my many good ideas which never saw the light of day.

By the late 1980s, it became clear that we didn't have the support needed to keep Women Strike for Peace functioning and we were forced to close down. Ethel was a sculptor and when the WSP office closed she gave me a beautiful small statue of a mother and child. Motherhood was a major focus of the early WSP program.

I know of two books about WSP. One is Ethel's book, *We Made a Difference* (and indeed they had) and the other book is *Women Strike for Peace: Traditional Motherhood and Radical Politics in the 1960s* by Amy Swerdlow. It presented a fascinating political background. Apparently, many WSP women were more radical than the organization, and they moderated their political expression in order to fit in with WSP and help build it.

In 1990, soon after the WSP office closed, I became the Director of the U.S. Peace Council. I knew Mike Myerson, then the Director, was retiring and they were looking for someone. I knew it was a multi-issue organization: pro-union, anti-racist, pro-prisoner rights, you name it. They were part of the World Peace Council, which had a lot of Socialist Countries supporting it, and their politics and mine were a good fit.

They were thrilled that I wanted to do the job, but the national office was in New York. They moved everything to Philadelphia! We kept the same nice office WSP had at 19th and Chestnut.

My work as Director of the U.S. Peace Council was similar to the work I'd been doing for decades. I saw to it that we had a newsletter go out to the members. I traveled to meet with local Peace Council groups and represented them at national peace meetings. We collaborated with the United States Conference of Mayors on planning a demonstration in Washington about money for cities, not for war. That was very exciting.

One time I was at a local Philadelphia peace group meeting, and the members were looking for a place to meet. I offered them our Peace Council office. It was wonderful. They paid for their use of the phone and copy machine, but we didn't charge them rent. We had a lot of young people there doing local activities. Many of them remained my friends long after the Peace Council office closed.

At some point we advertised for an intern. Marge Neidda was completing her Master's in social work at Temple University. She got all dressed up for the interview—unlike the rest of us! We really liked her, but we let her know it was an unpaid internship. After the interview, she said she would let us know, but she was so impressive we thought we wouldn't hear from her again. She called the next day, and it turned out her interest went well beyond peace. The volunteers and Marge and I got together for years afterwards, until COVID-19 kept us in our own homes.

Unfortunately, my role with the U.S. Peace Council didn't last very long. As it turned out, there was no money. I raised enough for mailings and to pay the rent, but we didn't have an angel like Ethel Taylor, so I never got paid. I laugh because I was the Director and didn't get paid; we also had an intern who didn't get paid and of course the volunteers didn't get paid. That was my last job in the peace and justice movement, but I remained active in various peace groups just as I always had.

After my leadership jobs in the peace movement, I found a job with the Jewish Children's Folkshul as a teacher and then principal. Folkshul is Yiddish for "Peoples' School." It is a long-standing venerable institution in Philadelphia, run by the parents. Both the principal and the School Board reflected the culture of the school—in terms of how Jewish, how secular, and how activist they were.

I had a few successful years as principal. I presided over a growth of membership, helped to develop creative teaching methods, and introduced Jewish customs unknown to the other members. However, I was sometimes at odds with some members of the school community. I challenged mainstream thinking and encouraged students to question everything, even the things they were told by teachers.

During our school Passover celebration, I explained why I put an orange on the Seder plate. In 1979, a Rabbi minimized the role of lesbians in the Jewish community, comparing their contributions to bread on a Seder plate; in other words that they didn't belong. Some women then put crusts of bread on the Seder plate as a protest. Others wanted to honor the idea but couldn't bring themselves to use bread, as only unleavened bread (like matzos) is allowed during Passover. So, they substituted an orange. After the program was over, a parent-teacher severely chastised me. She told me: "The kids are too young to hear about that." It was the 1990s and I thought it was about time we talked about it.

I again ruffled feathers when I threw my support behind a petition by the local Bar Association looking for organizations to support its campaign to ban capital punishment until it could be proven that racism did not play a role in how it was carried out. At a Folkshul Board meeting, I recommended our school sign on and thought it would be a foregone conclusion. My request was denied because one parent-teacher said it was too controversial an issue to be decided by the board—all of the parents needed to vote on it. I was taken aback but set my energies on gaining parent support. I made dozens of calls to ensure that parents who supported the petition would be at the next parents' meeting. We were successful and voted to support the ban, but I also realized that my priorities did not sit well with some of the parents. They didn't agree with my understanding of traditional secular culture; including the theme that since we can't depend on a god to solve the world's problems, it's up to us to do the work. The growing distance between some board members (and parents) and myself made me uncomfortable and I resigned soon after.

My last experience in Jewish education was mentoring a girl for her secular bat mitzvah. The girl was very smart, creative, and independent. While I worked with her for a short time, another person helped plan the actual bat mitzvah. Mort and I attended the ceremony, and I was asked to read a moving poem, "Blessed is the Match," by Chana Senesh.

Senesh was Hungarian-born but lived in British-mandated Palestine. Working with the British Army, she parachuted into Nazi-occupied European countries to contact underground movements, carry out intelligence work, operate secret wireless stations, and rescue Jews and others. Trying to cross from Yugoslavia into Hungary, she was arrested, tortured, and executed. She was twenty-three years old.

The story of the poem is that right before crossing the border into Hungary, Senesh handed a piece of paper to a comrade. On it was the poem, Ashrei Ha-Gashrur, "Blessed is the Match." Despite Chana Senesh's grim end, I found the poem to be inspirational. It begins:

Blessed is the match that was burned and ignited flames![1]

The bat mitzvah ceremony was held in the Calvary Methodist Church. The Christian religious objects in the church were covered over. The girl's mother spoke about her daughter, we sang Yiddish songs, and a moving play was read, "Seven Jewish Children" by a British playwright, Caryl Churchill. In it, seven people discuss how to teach their children about complex events in Jewish history, from the Holocaust to the creation of Israel to the violence in Gaza. It was a very moving and meaningful ceremony that matched my own understanding of secular Judaism.

•

Before I needed a walker, I continued going to rallies and demonstrations for many years. I remember one time giving out leaflets as part of a national demonstration, in front of a place that sold sweatshop clothes. I loved working with the union activists and allies. It was refreshing, giving out leaflets instead of sitting in an office at the typewriter or at meetings. It was bitter cold, and my husband didn't join us until near

---

1 https://jwa.org/thisweek/sep/02/2012/long-lost-poem-by-war-heroine-hannah-szenes-is-found

the end of the day since he is extremely vulnerable to the cold. Instead, Mort spent his time worrying about me. He needn't have been concerned—I wasn't cold, and my feet hadn't hurt! I'd been distributing leaflets without gloves and the adrenaline kept me warm. I loved it. I miss going to rallies and demonstrations. It was always energizing to work alongside people to accomplish things together. Even watching school bands, I'm enthralled seeing people work together to produce something beautiful.

Conclusion

I had to spend a week in the hospital and three months in a rehab center after falling and breaking my right leg in two places. This was from March 19 through July 8, 2020, at the beginning of the worldwide COVID pandemic. Most of the rehab stay was awful—I was isolated, immobile, and dependent on others—but I distinctly remember a few bright moments.

I worked with a wonderful group of young physical therapists several times a week. While I'm still reliant on a walker, even that would not have been possible without their sensitive, encouraging, and non-patronizing approach. The group included one white man and three Black women. I loved them. Early in the treatment, they asked me what work I'd done before I retired. I replied with my standard answer: two simultaneous careers. One as a teacher or administrator in a variety of Hebrew and Jewish schools; the other working as a volunteer and then professional peace and justice activist. When they asked what a peace and justice activist does, I told them about the time our mixed youth group of Black and white people was chased out of Youngstown, Ohio by the cops and warned to never come back because we tried to integrate a public swimming pool there. One of the Black female therapists came up to me, put her hand on my arm and quietly said, "Thank you for helping us."

I had never thought about thanks, had never pursued it,

had never received it, and I was tremendously moved. I was reminded of an exchange about seventy years ago, when my mother objected to my activism. In an effort to dissuade, she said, "They don't appreciate it anyway." But here was my therapist, genuinely touched by what we had done all those years ago.

In rehab, I also had a chance to reflect on where I got my radical ideas. I can't trace these ideas to my parents; they were always worrying about me and cautioning me not to push against society too hard. The closest I've come to determining the source of my ideas was that I took seriously the part of Jewish teaching to "act justly, love mercy and walk humbly . . ." (Micah 6:8) (Well, maybe not the "humbly" part.) I wanted others to experience the same advantages I had, and I wanted those rights to be acquired peacefully through perseverance. I like to think the work my comrades and I did through the decades made a difference. "There is a crack in everything. That's how the light gets in." (*Anthem*, Leonard Cohen)

A Final Note from Libby Frank

Dear Reader,

I thought I had completed writing this book. It was in the hands of the publisher, with as many stories, anecdotes, and memories as I could recall. I was finished.

And then my beloved husband—Dr. Morton H. Frank—died on October 21, 2023. We were married 67 years and he was just a few weeks short of his 96th birthday. My book was not complete. He was an incredibly loving, powerful, and integral part of my life and I needed to tell you that.

Mort suffered many years from developing dementia and other ailments.

He was an exceptional husband and father. Until 10-15 years ago, I assumed that all husbands/life partners of activists shared each other's complete lives, like Mort and I did. Dinner time wasn't just for eating, but for sharing the day's activities: problems, successes, and ideas (including with our sons, Alan and Reuben.)

Mort and I had an important similarity in our background—we were each raised in a traditional Jewish family which included being Zionists. Like me, Mort developed into a secular Jewish activist.

However, there was a major dissimilarity in our histories: Mort's father died when Mort was 6 years old and his mother had to take over his insurance business in order to support herself and her young son. She saw to it that Mort graduated from Bowdoin College (with a full scholarship) and he continued with advanced coursework to gain a PhD in Physiology. He conducted creative research and taught at a variety of colleges and universities.

Mort's family and research were important parts of his life. But he couldn't let the evils of the world go by. As you learned earlier in the book, he organized a huge rally in Philadelphia opposing U.S. missiles going to Germany. He also produced a local peace and justice calendar and did much more. His dry humor will be missed by many.

Goodnight, beloved Comrade.

A Final Note from Heather Shafter

Dear Reader,

I too thought that I had completed writing this book. It was edited and proofread. All of the pictures were added and captioned. And then, on December 12, 2023, Libby Frank passed away unexpectedly. It was heartbreaking to work so long together on this book only to have Libby miss seeing its publication.

The evening I learned that Libby was gone, I could not stop thinking about her or this book. I stayed up most of the night and many thoughts occurred to me. I'd like to share two of them with you.

First, I thought about what is happening in the world right now. Israel and Hamas are at war. The hope for peace in the Middle East feels very distant. I remembered all the work Libby and her co-activists did over the past few decades. Why do we have so much violence in the Middle East after everything they did? Why wasn't it enough? The answer that came to me is that peace and justice work is not something that is ever complete. Every generation must have its activists because every generation will have its oppressors.

Second, that is why stories like these are so important. We find inspiration from the people who come before us and we learn from them. We repurpose what's been done before to create new ways of challenging violence and oppression. When we are effective, then history—instead of being a circle that forever repeats—can be a spiral that elevates humanity just a little more through the generations.

Libby, you lived a long, full, and powerful life. You impacted the lives and ideas of so many people! Your work is done, but your story will continue to inspire people to work for peace and justice.

Goodnight, dear friend and mentor.

Acknowledgements

Libby and Heather are grateful to the following individuals and groups who contributed mightily to making this book possible. Many sent checks; some brought us food; some gave money to help pay for Libby's compassionate aides who cleared the way for her to think, write and edit; (too) many suggested book titles; some took the checks to the bank for deposit; those who provided encouragement, such as requesting advanced copies; a few whined, "are you still working on that book?" And to those I forgot to name, please add your name.

Adina Abramowitz, Barbara Armentrout, Emily Batdorf, Michael Blackman, Shoshana Bricklin, Melissa Bridge, Jeremy Brochin, Tura Cook, Teri Cox, Elena Detoma, Theresa Diamond, Bonney DosSantos, Joanne Dowd, Judy Elson, Toby Emmer, Leonard & Helen Evelev, Tina Exarhos, Rachel Falkove, Helen Feinberg, Alan Frank, Jan Fritz, Jean Gajary, Terry Galpin-Plattner, Susan Halfond, Lynne Jacobs, Donald Joseph, Naomi Klayman, Louise Lisi, Janice Marie, Joan Martini, Evonne Marzouk, Marc Mauer, Michael Mauer, Ellen Miades, Jane Miades, Dirk Moore, Lynne Moore, Karen Perez, Judy Rubin, Allison Sacks, Theresa Savage, Mary Jane Schutzius, David Shafter, Joanne Shafter, Debra Siegel, Michael Silver, Gayle Simons, George Stern, Dolores Taller, Betsy Teutsch, Nadine Wagenhoffer, Rivkah Walton, Deborah Weinstein, Jennifer Weston, Morissa Wiser.

We'd also like to acknowledge the Swarthmore Peace Archives for curating a history of peace and justice work though articles, documents, and photos. These files were valuable in corroborating dates and providing additional details about some of the events described in this book. Lastly, we'd like to acknowledge the Philadelphia Chapter of the Women's International League for Peace and Freedom for their support.

About the Authors

Libby Frank had her first paid job in peace work as Director of the Bergen County Peace Center in NJ (1969-1973). Her next peace job was as Executive Director of the U.S. section of WILPF (1981-1986). Prior to that, she held a variety of leadership positions such as chair of the WILPF Childhood Education Committee (1965-1969), founder and chair of the WILPF Middle East Committee (1973-1981), and leader of the WILPF Middle East Delegation (1978). As a result of her peace and justice work, Libby Frank has been the subject of television, radio, and news articles over her decades of activism. She has delivered countless speeches around the country and globally on the topics of peace, justice, and the Middle East.

Heather Shafter completed two internships with WILPF (U.S. National Office and France National Office) and participated in the local Philadelphia chapter for many years afterwards. During that time, she had a term as branch Coordinator and Membership Coordinator. Heather currently works as the COO of BRODY Professional Development, a communication skills training company. Heather was credited for her editorial contributions to two published books: *Impact: Deliver Presentations That Get Results* by Marjorie Brody, and the Young Adult novel *The Prophetess* by Evonne Marzouk.

Index